Literary Cafés of Paris

LITERARY
CAFÉS
OF
PARIS

Noël Riley Fitch

STARRHILL PRESS
Washington & Philadelphia

Dedicated to Gailyn Fitch, café sitter *par excellence*

Starrhill Press, publisher
P.O. Box 32342
Washington, D.C. 20007
(202) 686-6703

Illustrations by Jonel Sofian.
Maps by Deb Norman.
Hand-marbled paper by Iris Nevins, Sussex, N.J.

Library of Congress Cataloging in Publication Data

    Fitch, Noël Riley, 1937–   .
       Literary cafés of Paris / Noël Riley Fitch. — 1st ed.
      p.   cm.
    Bibliography: p.
    Includes index.
    ISBN 0-913515-42-6 : $7.95
    1. Literary landmarks—France—Paris. 2. Hotels, taverns, etc.-
-France— Paris. 3. Restaurants, lunch rooms, etc.—France—Paris.
4. Authors, French—Homes and haunts—France—Paris. 5. French
literature—France—Paris—History and criticism. 6. Authors—Homes
and haunts—France—Paris. 7. Paris (France)—Social life and
customs. 8. Paris (France)—Intellectual life. I. Title.
PQ148.F5   1989
914.4'36'0488—dc19   88-32399
                                                         CIP

Printed in the United States of America
First edition
9 8 7 6 5 4

Contents

La Palette

Foreword

France is the land where dalliance
is so passionately understood.
       – Arnold Bennett

The primary requisite for writing about the literary life of the cafés of Paris is not a taste for wine *per se* but a love of literary history and a history of café-sitting. I was smitten by Paris twenty years ago when in my mind the city was the bohemian myth of living in a cold garret and writing on a café terrace facing a blazing brazier—flushed in the forehead, where lie the memory and the imagination, freezing on the backside, where mere physical support rests. During the intervening years I have explored the reality of Parisian artistic life—focusing, because I am a foreigner here, on the foreign artists in this city, and falling in love with a man who might well be French, though he was born in Berlin and reared in Manhattan. We have a *pied-à-terre* on the street that divides the 6th and 7th *arrondissements* in this city of our estival choice. Like Waverley Root (*The Food of France*), that American food lover from my mother's home state of Rhode Island, we feast on the bounty of France. My brother-in-law writes from Idaho to ask if I do anything but eat. I walk between meals or sit in cafés waiting for mealtime.

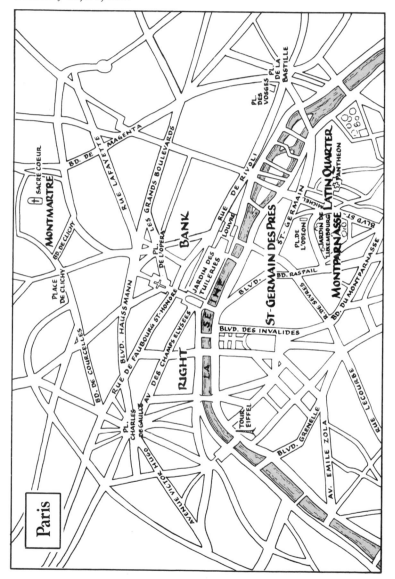

Café Life in Paris

I F THE FRENCH, as Henry James believed, have excelled in the art of living—in what they call *l'entente de la vie*—one of the most visible manifestations of this art is the café. Here one can sit in peace for hours, not hassled by impatient waiters or waiting customers. Here one can read and write in the morning, conduct business in the afternoon, and laugh and argue with friends at night.

Part of the pleasure and excitement of café life lies in the bright colors, the play of life, and the fusion of odors. Thomas Wolfe, in *Of Time and the River,* describes the "corrupt and sensual, subtle and obscene" intoxication of odors in Parisian cafés. He thought the mélange could be described as a compact of "the smells of costly perfumes, of wine, beer, brandy, and of the acrid and nostalgic fumes of French tobacco, of roasted chestnuts, black French coffee, mysterious liquors of a hundred brilliant and intoxicating colors, and the luxurious flesh of scented women."

But the poetry and odors, the Gauloises and expresso, are not the only explanation for the centrality of the café in the texture of French life. Cafés provide some of the basic necessities of life: coffee, cigarettes, toilets, newspapers and telephones. Add stamps and postcards, which you find in a *café tabac,* a convenient sidewalk seat and, most essential, a comfortable environment where you will not be reminded of the hour. Contrast this to the United States, where thirst is quenched at a public drinking fountain or bustling coffee shop and where flights of fancy are brought to earth by a clock, perhaps chiming every quarter hour.

The café is closely related to, and sometimes difficult to distinguish from, the coffee house of Austria, the taverna of Greece, the club and pub of England, the bar or coffee shop of America. But it is neither a bar nor a restaurant. It is a lounging place, where one meets friends and exchanges news while having a drink or a bite of food. Cafés first appeared in Paris after tea, chocolate and coffee were introduced to the cabarets in the second half of the 17th century. The cabarets subsequently opened their windows and doors to the street, added crystal chandeliers, introduced the habit of smoking with coffee and provided leading journals to read. The first Paris café was probably Le Procope, opened about 1675 (it moved to its present location in 1686) by a Sicilian, who helped turn France into a coffee-drinking society.

The handful of cafés in 1675 had grown in number to 1100 by the beginning of the Revolution. In the 19th century the numbers continued to climb: 3,000 in 1825, 4,000 in 1869, until they reached a peak between the two World Wars. The great cafés of the 19th century were on the *Grands Boulevards*—handsome establishments with plate glass, gilded ceilings, blazing lights: Café de la Régence, Café de la Paix, Café Anglais. At the beginning of the 20th century there were many artists' cafés in Montmartre, but the trail soon led to Montparnasse and after the Second World War to St-Germain-des-Prés. By that time the numbers had begun to diminish. Although many Parisians still found restaurants affordable, television and improved living quarters changed their eating habits. Even today, when far more Parisians eat at home, they often have their coffee at a café.

Café-sitting has a daily rhythm. Coffee and croissant at the Dôme charges the batteries for a morning of writing, attending art classes, museum visiting or banking. One may meet a friend at Brasserie Lipp for lunch at 1 p.m. An afternoon of work and then the writer is at the Deux-Magots nursing an apéritif. During the early evening of bustling social activity around the St-Germain-des-Prés Square, groups come and go from the table. Waverley Root called the reshuffling "intramural movement." Sometime between

8 and 9 a dinner group forms to eat at a small restaurant. Coffee ends the evening at the Closerie des Lilas. New groups form and break up all evening long; the nightcap can last for hours.

Wasted time? Certainly not. Idle time? In part. There is time to sit and contemplate, to dream and observe life. Time to plan the next story or the word order of a poem. Time to overhear a conversation or capture the rhythm of dialogue for a play. Even the noisy, crowded moments nourish art and literature, because cafés bring together artists for companionship, inspiration, influence and business. No wonder that from Rabelais to Verlaine, to Sartre and Beauvoir, writers have thrived on café life.

Cafés have one mask for summer, another for winter. They turn outward in summer, inward in winter. In the months of cold rain, the cafés are a warm haven. The writers gather inside or on the terraces behind glass partitions that protect them from rain and sleet and are heated by braziers. These once burned a fuel that crackled like firecrackers, glowed red hot and emitted a rather pleasant odor. Today's electric braziers still glow hot near the coats and galoshes huddled by the entrance. Cigarette smoke in a crowded café in winter can make you asthmatic, but everyone is far warmer than in their badly heated apartments and cold hotel rooms. Summer is heralded by the unfolding of the cafés, which spill their tables into the sidewalk. Now outdoor life begins. Faces and extended legs rotate with the sun. For Henry James, summer boulevards became "a long chain of cafés, each one with its little promontory of chairs and tables projecting into the sea of asphalt. These promontories are doubtless not exactly islands of the blessed, peopled though some of them may be with sirens addicted to beer, but they may help you pass a hot evening."

In a city of apartment dwellers, the café has traditionally served as an extension of the apartment, as its living and family room. "As I was a teacher and hadn't much money I lived in a hotel," wrote Jean-Paul Sartre, "and like all people who live in hotels I spent most of the day in cafés." French apartments are small; the social system has historically allotted 45 percent of the income for food and only 10 to 20 percent for rent. With small living areas and high heating costs, it is not surprising that the French have customarily invited guests out to eat in a restaurant and have finished the meal with coffee in a café.

In the same way, cafés have served as studies or offices for writers, who can eat, drink, receive friends and work all in one place. And for the price of one coffee the writer has a heated room for the day. The café becomes an extension of home and family, a place where one is known and welcomed. "I have the sense of being part of a family, and that protects one against depression," Simone de Beauvoir says of café life during the war.

Almost every French or expatriate writer and artist serves an apprenticeship in one Paris café or another. Simone de Beauvoir wrote upstairs in the Sélect. Ernest Hemingway wrote short stories in the Closerie des Lilas. Léon-Paul Fargue spent early evening and late night of every day in the café of his choice, first Café de Flore and, in the last years of his life, Café François Coppée.

An open-air café gives a writer a sense of the world and clears his head of library mothballs and the "smell of literature," says Anatole Broyard in the *New York Times.* Gertrude Stein shunned cafés, he explains with amusement, and "that may be the trouble with her work; nobody in a café, even for free drinks, would have sat still for all those repetitions."

One of the most memorable scenes in Ernest Hemingway's account of his Parisian years, *A Moveable Feast,* occurs in the first pages when he stops in a café in the Place St-Michel, hangs up his wet raincoat, puts his worn hat on the rack, orders a *café au lait,* takes out his notebook and pencil and writes a story set in upper Michigan. He captures the warm and friendly atmosphere (warmed further by a Martinique rum) and the inspiration of a pretty girl sitting alone by the window. She excites him and he writes on to the finish. When he looks up, she is gone. Feeling empty—as after making love, he notes—and both sad and happy to have the story finished, he orders oysters and cold white wine. He soon loses the empty feeling.

Because of the hours spent writing in cafés, each writer develops a loyalty for and an identification with a particular café. It is easier to change one's religion than one's café. Even if you do not know where a friend lives, you always know his café. A few writers—such as poet Paul Fort at the Closerie des Lilas or Sartre at the Sélect were kings who held court over constantly changing vassals.

Other writers use several cafés. Apollinaire, the charismatic poet who lived only 38 years, lunched at La Palette, took coffee at the Flore, and never missed Paul Fort's Tuesday meetings at the Closerie des Lilas during the first decade of this century. For some writers, working and meeting friends in a café, where alcohol is an inevitable attraction, led to ruin. Paul Verlaine, lyric vagabond poet of the 19th century, spent his life in cafés drinking the poisonous absinthe and wandering drunkenly from hospital to prison in deteriorating health until he died alone and wretched.

In addition to serving the valuable function of studio and office, cafés are centers for the dissemination of gossip. Ernest Hemingway, himself a newspaperman, said that the cafés of Montparnasse "anticipated the columnist as the daily substitute for

La Coupole

immortality." Léon-Paul Fargue, the poet of Paris, earlier said the same thing about the St-Germain-des-Prés cafés:

> If during the day there is a meeting of the French Cabinet, a boxing match in New Jersey, a grand prize for conformists, a literary splash, a celebrity contest on the Right Bank or a shouting match, café-goers of Place St-Germain-des-Prés are the first to hear the results of these encounters and competitions. . . . [Here] one feels the most up to date, the closest to real events, to the people who know the real truths about the nations, the world and art.

He particularly liked Lipp, where "for the price of a beer, you can get a complete rundown on the day's happenings in Paris."

Not surprisingly, the modern newspaper has its roots in the 17th-century coffee houses of London—social centers which Addison visited to sample public opinion for the *Spectator.*

> So great a Universitie
> I think there ne'er was any
> In which you may a scholar be
> For spending of a Penny
> > —News from a Coffee-House
> > (English broadside of 1677)

In French cafés, newspapers have traditionally been available, and the newswriters themselves gather there to collect and disseminate information. Emile Zola wrote his great essay, "J'accuse," an indictment of the French government's handling of the Dreyfus affair, at a table in Durand's. "J'accuse" was published in *L'Aurore,* and the next day the paper was mounted on wooden rods and read at every café table in Paris.

Though inflation and the development of the modern newspaper have changed the economy of the news, the modern café continues to be a platform for political and literary criticism and debate. It sometimes serves the functions that formerly resided in the church, university and town square. Intellectual life, according to Richard Le Gallienne (*From a Paris Garret*) in 1936, moved to public cafés: "These wildly-lit cafés, turbulent and tumultuous, are the direct descendants of the cloisters of Notre-Dame and Sainte-Geneviève." Political life also fomented there: one of the speeches that precipitated the fall of the Bastille was delivered outside the Café Foy in the Palais-Royal; during the Algerian war, anti-Gaullist students spilled out of the cafés of St-Germain des Prés, pulled cobblestones from the street and hurled them at elegant cars passing in the street.

That the café is a literary as well as a political forum, you will see in the specific descriptions that follow. Sisley Huddleston, an English journalist in Paris in the 1920s and 1930s, said that the café in France is the "forcing ground of art and literature." According to Roger Shattuck (*The Banquet Years*), Impressionism was "the first artistic movement entirely organized in cafés"—cafés such as the Nouvelle Athènes and the Guerbois. The Dada movement began in a Zurich café with Tristan Tzara. Editors of the little magazines of the 1920s "went to the Dôme in search of contributors," writes American critic Malcolm Cowley. "It was easier than writing letters . . . for, in addition to its other functions, the Dôme was an over-the-table market that dealt in literary futures." The café as literary forum is best seen in the life of Jean-Paul Sartre, the leading intellectual of his time in France. Sartre, who insisted on the public role of the writer, used the café for political exchange of ideas. Unlike any other country, all of French culture is concentrated in one city, Paris. Everyone reads the same papers and goes to the same cafés, where issues of culture and politics are debated on neutral ground.

The café also plays a role in business and commerce. Here vendors sell their newspapers, magazines, shoddy art and knick-knacks; even prostitutes parade their goods. Sinclair Lewis claims that "there were a few professional prostitutes to be found at the Dôme or the Sélect, no matter how competent were some of the amateurs." On a more serious note, cafés are the best place for business and professional meetings: they are open long hours, food and drink are available, and they can be found in numerous convenient locations. In Paris, when one calls a friend or business associate to arrange a meeting, the first thought is to choose a central café. It is a public place, conducive to waiting, with a vantage point on the city and the promise of some diversion should the meeting be delayed.

Finally, café-sitting has great entertainment value. The café is theater and fashion. It is Kiki with her colorful face make-up; it is Josephine Baker strolling the aisles of La Coupole with a cheetah; it is Salvador Dali with curled mustache and cape sweeping into the Sélect. It is also sport. Back when the Dôme was a dingy place, it had a billiard room; chess has always been played inside the Sélect; and tea dancing was integral to the life of La Coupole.

Café-sitting affords another sport worth mentioning. People-watching from a café is the national pastime in France as is baseball in the United States. The field for this sport is important: one must choose the ground carefully, seeking comfortable surroundings near a busy street or intersection, just the right amount of sun, and enough loose change for at least one coffee. The best players choose a good sight-line both to pedestrians and to their fellow players. The object of the game is to identify passersby, by nationality and profession. Americans were once the easiest to recognize because of their broad stride and innocent faces. Professional people-watchers can quickly surmise entire life stories. There is only one rule in this game: never be caught staring.

A final word about change and time, provoked by the loud laments protesting the destruction of La Coupole in 1988. Cafés live and die or renew themselves now as always. Most of the cafés presented in this book have undergone a succession of transforma-tions, and with each the habitués have deplored the change. Hemingway returned to Paris in 1924 to find La Closerie des Lilas tarted up, and the waiters without their mustaches. He was chagrined. Harold Stearns, one of the most notorious American newspapermen in Paris in the 1920s, remembers when the Dôme was an old-fashioned corner bistro, the Sélect an old furniture shop, La Coupole a coal-and-wood yard, the Dingo a tiny workmen's café, and the Rotonde the "small and dirty and historical" place where Trotsky hung out. One newspaperman remarked in 1933 that he had seen the Coupole expand over the quarter "like a mushroom," the Sélect "go Oscar Wilde and the Rotonde Nordic," and the Dôme evolve from "an ugly wart" to an "American bar. . . . I've seen it all." When change occurs, remember that the visuals are transitory and the ugly new red plush will eventually fade; the spirit of the café, where one is welcome each day and can work or meet friends, is perpetual, if not eternal. The popularity of individual cafés has always waxed and waned; as one café becomes a favorite, another is declared "dead"; and the rhythm continues.

The cafés discussed in the following pages are all alive today. Some of the great old cafés that have disappeared will be mentioned in the brief introductions to the districts where they were. Cafés associated with only one writer are not included: Gide's favorite Restaurant des Saints-Pères, Samuel Beckett's Café de l'Arrivée where he wrote *Proust* in 1931, Adamov's Old Navy Bar where he spent every day from 1964 to 1967, John Dos Passos's Au Rendezvous des Mariniers (now gone) on the Quai d'Anjou, and Colette's Grand Véfour. Nor are places such as Maxim's which, though used in the setting of several plays and musicals, is chiefly a society restaurant. Other cafés are fixed only in fiction, such as Café Momus in Henri Murger's *Scenes de la Vie de Bohème*, which inspired Puccini's opera, *La Bohème* (1896). A handful of bars and restaurants rich in literary history are discussed briefly among the cafés.

> "The hours I have spent in cafés are the
> only ones I call living, apart from writing."
>
> — Anaïs Nin

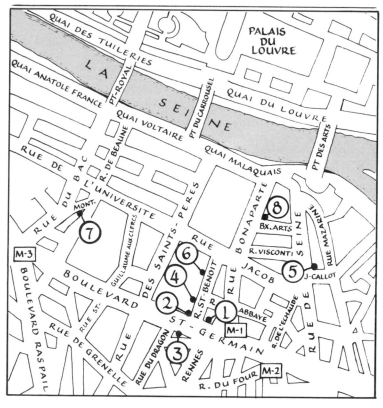

St-Germain-des-Prés

1. Café des Deux-Magots
2. Café de Flore
3. Brasserie Lipp
4. Le Montana
5. La Palette
6. Le Petit Saint-Benoît
7. Bar du Pont-Royal
8. Restaurant des Beaux-Arts

Metro stops:

M-1. St-Germain-des-Prés
M-2. Mabillon
M-3. Rue du Bac

Cafés of St-Germain-des-Prés

CAFÉS AT major street intersections are popular because of their accessibility and the perspective they offer—one has a greater chance to see one's friends. Consider the following three cafés located at the junctions of several streets and boulevards: Deux-Magots (St-Germain and Rennes), Closerie des Lilas (Montparnasse, Notre-Dame-des-Champs, L'Observatoire, Port-Royal), and the Dôme (Montparnasse, Delambre, Raspail). Each one has a view of several confluent passages, and each sits within steps of a métro stop (St-Germain-des-Prés, Port-Royal and Vavin, respectively) and several bus stops.

The Deux-Magots and its neighboring cafés are located just south of the Seine River near Abbaye St-Germain, the oldest church of Paris. Today this is a neighborhood of art schools, art shops, galleries and publishing houses. Its cafés are associated in the minds of contemporary readers with Sartre and the French existentialists.

Yet a century before these philosophers took possession of the Flore, Delacroix had his studio nearby in a dingy courtyard; his good friend Chopin installed a piano in the studio and gave musical evenings with George Sand as guest of honor; Victor Hugo lived and worked in Rue du Dragon; Racine died in 1699 in Rue Visconti, the same street where Balzac failed as a book printer in 1828; and Oscar Wilde died, in exile, in Rue des Beaux-Arts in 1900. This quarter is rich in literary associations. "The streets sing, the stones talk. The houses drip history, glory, romance," Henry Miller wrote from the Hôtel St-Germain-des-Prés in 1930.

CAFÉ DES DEUX-MAGOTS

170 Boulevard St-Germain (6e) Tel: 45.48.55.25
Open: every day, 8 a.m. to 2 a.m.
Métro: St-Germain-des-Prés

Founded in 1875 at one of the best locations in Paris, the Deux-Magots sprawls out into one of the broadest and busiest intersections of the city and offers a full view of the ancient church across the street. There are at least two stories that explain the name and origin of Deux-Magots: one claims it took the name from a hat shop on the same site, another that it was once a business dealing in oriental merchandise whose trademark was two grotesque Chinese porcelain figures (magots). You can find the Chinese dignitaries on the center posts inside, where the tables beneath the large mirrors offer quiet sitting.

For more than a hundred years this has been the home of writers, many of whom wrote their books here, organized their manuscripts inside on a table, or celebrated with their editors upon publication. *"Rendez-vous de l'élite intellectuelle,"* reads the menu, as if to compensate for the high prices. Even fifty years ago, Léon-Paul Fargue, that French poet of the streets, complained that the café is "much admired by snobs who find that Dubonnet at 110 sous is not an exaggerated expenditure for one who wishes to be present at the modern writers' cocktail hour." Between the wars, before German tourists poured in and prices went too high, dramatist Jean Giraudoux breakfasted here every morning and held court for his friends. Poets Verlaine, Rimbaud and Mallarmé in the 19th century, and surrealists Breton and Artaud early in this century, hung out here as well.

One August evening in 1926, Grant Wood, who had studied and painted in Europe on several occasions, confided to his friend William Shirer, an American newsman for the Chicago *Tribune,* that he was going home to Iowa. While sipping white wine and gazing at the tower of the church, he explained that "everything" he had done "up to now was wrong," and all the landscapes he had painted had been done by the French Impressionists hundreds of times before and a hundred times better! Over Shirer's protests, Wood announced, "I've learned something. . . . All I really know is home—Iowa!" He would go home and "paint those damn cows and barns and barnyards and cornfields and little red schoolhouses and all those pinched faces." When they broke at midnight, Wood had made a decision that would secure his career as an American artist. When his *American Gothic*—with his sister and his dentist as models—appeared in the annual exhibition of the Chicago Art Institute in 1930, Grant Wood suddenly burst into national fame with his portraits of American life.

A hundred stories could be told of encounter, discovery and creation at the Deux-Magots. English poet Arthur Symons wrote "The Absinthe Drinker" here. Simone de Beauvoir worked on a novel and read Hegel here, but she also admits to writer's block: "I sat in the Deux-Magots and gazed at the blank sheet of paper in front of me. I felt the need to write in my fingertips, and the taste of the words in my throat, but I didn't know where to start, or what." A small group of Americans that included Malcolm Cowley, Matthew Josephson and Robert Coates met here to plan their little review *Sucession* (1922–1924). And Louis Aragon, André Breton and Philippe Soupault often sat here in the 1920s formulating their *Surrealist Manifestos*.

Many have recorded significant meetings at the Deux-Magots. Picasso met Dora Maar, probably the most intelligent woman in his life, here. She was a photographer who became his lover and model but refused to live with him. A sculpture of her head stands in the garden across the street and next to the church. Here also Eugene Jolas introduced the Americans Hart Crane and Harry Crosby. Crosby published Crane's *The Bridge* at his Black Sun Press nearby in the Place de Fürstemberg. Gore Vidal met Christopher Isherwood here and they became fast friends, each dedicating a book to the other: Isherwood's *A Single Man* and Vidal's *Myra Breckinridge*.

Hundreds of writers have lived within steps of the Deux-Magots. During his 46th and last year of life, while living in the

Rue des Beaux-Arts, Oscar Wilde had coffee and a roll each morning and sipped absinthe (wormwood, now illegal) each evening on the terrace. Djuna Barnes (*Nightwood*) lived around the corner in the 1920s and drank here often, as did Janet Flanner (Genêt of *New Yorker* fame) who lived in the Hôtel St-Germain-des-Prés. Flanner told of meeting with fellow journalist Hemingway at a back table where they discussed the suicides of their fathers and agreed that if either one ever killed himself "the other was not to grieve but to remember that liberty could be as important in the acts of dying as in the acts of living." Kathryn Hulme (*The Nun's Story*), who lived in the same hotel as Flanner and Henry Miller in Rue Bonaparte, says she learned how to "add seltzer at widely placed intervals" to her vermouth-cassis in order to make it "last for hours on the *terrace* of the Deux-Magots."

Le Café des Deux-Magots

CAFÉ DE FLORE
172 Boulevard St-Germain (6e) Tel: 45.48.55.26
Open: 8 a.m. to 1:30 a.m.
Métro: St-Germain-des-Prés

"This afternoon I'm upstairs at the Flore, near the window; I can see the wet street, the plane tree swaying in the sharp wind; there are a lot of people, and downstairs there's a great hubbub." So wrote Simone de Beauvoir in the late 1940s, on one of the many days that she worked at a table at the Flore. She wrote portions of her journal, *Second Sex* and novels such as *The Mandarins* in this venerable neighborhood café. Flore was founded in 1865 and named for a small statue of Flore, the goddess of flowers and mother of spring, that once stood in front of the door.

The café is homey, with its worn Art Deco interior of red banquettes, mahogany and mirrors. Outside it is characterized by cream-colored awnings with green and gold letters and by its location on the corner of two busy streets: the little Rue St-Benoît is crowded with foot traffic in the evenings when the restaurants are full; on the wide boulevard, the Flore sits between an excellent postcard shop and a distinguished bookstore, La Hune, next to the Deux-Magots.

Beginning with Huysmans and Remy de Gourmont in the late 19th century, nearly every French writer has spent time at the Flore. Yet the Flore has been identified with several distinct groups at different times, and each one has in turn determined the personality of the café. One of the first significant groups to make the Flore home was the political Right. L'Action Française wrote its first manifestos here in 1899 (they were printed nearby in Rue Cassette). The leader of L'Action Française was Charles Maurras, who lived at 60 Rue de Verneuil. He called his political memoirs *Souvenirs de vie politique: Au signe de Flore.*

In the first decade of this century, Apollinaire and his friends founded *Les Soirées de Paris* magazine here. The group that dominated the Flore environment in the following decade included Léon-Paul Fargue, André Breton and his Surrealist colleagues, and

Picasso. After he moved to live in his studio nearby in Rue des Grands-Augustins, Picasso patronized first the Deux-Magots. He moved to the Flore in the late 1930s, where he engaged in lengthy political discussions joined occasionally by Marc Chagall. At the end of an evening the two exiled artists would exchange the matchbooks on which each had doodled. Janet Flanner says she saw Picasso there every night after 1945, sitting at the second table in front of the main door, sipping a small bottle of mineral water and speaking with his Spanish friends.

In the late 1930s there was also a quiet group at the Flore whose fame would later burst forth to dominate a generation. Jean-Paul Sartre, who lived a few blocks away in the Hôtel La Louisiane (Rue de Seine), used this café as his study because it was heated. He had left the Montparnasse cafés because too many Nazis gathered there. By 1940, he says, "Simone de Beauvoir and I more or less set up house in the Flore," where they wrote from nine in the morning until noon, and then from four until eight in the evening. Their marble-top tables held inkwells, not drinks. They worked between the telephone and the toilet—"among drafts and questionable odors," one observer amusingly phrased it. It "was like home to us," added Sartre. "When the air raid alarm went off we would feign to leave and then climb up to the first floor and go on working."

Although they lived separately, Sartre and Beauvoir were lovers and philosophical mates throughout most of their adult lives. Warmed by a sawdust-burning stove in the Flore, they invented a philosophy expounded in Sartre's *L'Etre et le néant* which asserts that matter precedes the spirit, that man creates for himself a spirit through his own will and is master of his fate, but at the same time is completely alone. Certainly the aloneness was easier to bear in a French café.

The Flore was also the café of poet and screen writer, Jacques Prévert. A small man in dark clothes, he wore a black hat pushed back on his head and scribbled verse on menus, toilet paper and paper napkins. His droopy eyes made him look tired or sleepy, but he saw more than most. His satiric poems, scribbled at his table, were collected under the title *Paroles* and set to music by Joseph Kosma. When disciples began surrounding his table after the war, he left for the south of France. Beauvoir remembers that he had a large following who "worshiped his films and poetry, doing their best to ape his language and attitudes."

The man who watched the rise and departure of each literary hero was Boubal, the owner, who lived across the street until his death. Prévert once said that when a glass broke at the Flore, Boubal heard it from his bed. He watched with amused tolerance while the "Capri set," (the gays, whom he called *mes mignons*) took refuge at the Flore from harassment by the morals squad on the Champs-Elysées. Like every enduring café, the Flore commands the loyalty of dozens of newsmen, poets, film writers and nearby residents who visit daily.

Le Café de Flore

Brasserie Lipp

151 Boulevard St-Germain (6e) Tel: 45.48.53.91
Open: 8 a.m. to 12:45 a.m. (closed August)
Métro: St-Germain-des-Prés

"I go there as an Englishman to his club, sure to find each evening a true friend," wrote Léon-Paul Fargue, whose father and uncle designed and fired the ceramic tiles that still characterize the interior of Brasserie Lipp. "One couldn't write thirty lines in a newspaper, paint a picture, or hold reasonable political views without spending at least one evening a week in Lipp's."

Lipp stays true to its origins as a brasserie by serving Alsatian beer on tap and sausage with sauerkraut. Order any time of day or night from a menu considerably smaller than that of La Coupole, the larger brasserie of Montparnasse. At midday recently, I sat next to a Parisian couple at Lipp who dined on caviar, toast and white wine. We ate in front downstairs, where you can see everyone who enters.

Past the revolving door of Lipp today is the world of 1900—the authentic one, not the instant Belle Epoque that is now being recreated all over Paris. Old metal chandeliers illuminate high, painted ceilings and dark wood furniture. Century-old yellow, blue and green tiles depicting parrots, cranes and flowers surround large mirrors, which make the place seem larger than it is. Add leather banquettes, a boy selling *Le Monde* (the newspaper for serious reading, with few pictures) and professional waiters in black suits, bow ties, vests with pockets for tips, and white aprons from waist to shoe tops, and you know you have stepped into a Paris tradition.

When France lost Alsace to Germany in the war of 1870, many Alsatians migrated to Paris and opened brasseries, including Lipp and Florderer (Flo). Léonard Lipp (Fargue mistakenly calls him Lippman) named his brasserie after a famous eating establishment in Strasbourg, Brasserie des Bords du Rhin (On the Banks of the Rhine). Customers preferred to call it after the family that owned it. Madame Lipp was cashier, and you can still see the prominent cashier's stall at the center right downstairs. Marcellin Cazes bought Lipp in 1920, when there were only eight tables and two waiters. He expanded into the back and upstairs and in 1958 was given the Legion of Honor for running the best literary salon in Paris. By then Lipp was the choice of leading actresses, cabinet ministers, television personalities, Nobel Prize-winning writers and their publishers (Grasset, Gallimard and Hachette are nearby).

His son Roger Cazes, who managed the place until his death in 1987, used to tell reporters that his customers varied in the course of a day from businessmen in the morning and writers in the afternoon to actors, politicians and literary celebrities at night. Tourists are on the terrace at all times. The after-theater group orders oysters and white wine. For nearly a decade, on Friday nights at 10:50 after filming *Apostrophes*—that popular literary salon of the small screen—the television host Bernard Pivot, his visiting authors and their television team met upstairs near the radiator for supper.

Lipp has been the scene of various literary directorates. Earlier in this century Jean Paulhan and his *Nouvelle Revue Française* group made Lipp their headquarters. Then the Vieux-Colombier theater group, located just a few streets away, made their home here. And of course there was Fargue and his group which included Antoine de Saint-Exupéry, the author-aviator whose fable *Le Petit Prince* is often the first book read by foreign students studying French.

Lipp has long been a spot for politicians, including François Mitterrand who lives on the Left Bank. Located halfway between the Senate and the National Assembly, Lipp has remained open sometimes until 4 a.m. while the National Assembly argued late into the night. According to Waverley Root, the American journalist who wrote so knowledgeably of the food and wine of France, "a great deal of intrigue and extracurricular government activity used to take place chez Lipp."

Though most people have gone to Lipp's through the years less for the food than for the action, Ernest Hemingway made the food famous in an often quoted passage of his memoir, *A Moveable Feast*. In the 1920s, during one of the fasts he indulged in to heighten his perceptions (and because "hunger was good discipline"), he stopped by the Shakespeare and Company bookshop where the American proprietor Sylvia Beach insisted that he had better take care of himself and go immediately to lunch. He chose the Brasserie Lipp, where he sat on a bench against the wall with the mirror to his back and ordered potato salad and a large glass of beer—probably the *sérieux*, a giant glass stein:

> The beer was very cold and wonderful to drink. The *pommes à l'huile* were firm and marinated and the olive oil delicious. I ground black pepper over the potatoes and moistened the bread in the olive oil. After the first heavy draft of beer I drank and ate very slowly. When the *pommes à l'huile* were gone I ordered another serving of *cervelas*. This was a sausage like a heavy, wide frankfurter split in two and covered with a special mustard sauce.
>
> I mopped up all the oil and all of the sauce with bread and drank the beer slowly until it began to lose its coldness and then I finished it and ordered a *demi* . . .

The mirrors, mosaics, menu (and sausage) still await your visit today, but the food is not as good as Hemingway found it.

The history of Lipp is peppered with stories of political and literary quarrels. Harold Loeb, the editor of *Broom* magazine in the 1920s, remembers eating at Lipp one day after the publication of Hemingway's *The Sun Also Rises*. It humiliated and angered him to be identified as the model for Robert Cohn. Hemingway walked in through the revolving doors and both men, former friends, "grimaced" when he passed Loeb's table. Hemingway walked to the rear and sat with his back to Loeb, who "watched his neck go red. Then [Hemingway] walked out. We never spoke."

Gene Tunney and Thornton Wilder, the pugilist and the writer, were drinking together at Lipp when they were approached by a reporter for the *Chicago Tribune* (Paris edition). At first they denied who they were, then demanded to know, "Why can't you fellows ever let us alone?" Tunney said he was tired of publicity. When told that he should not have come to Lipp's, "a haunt of newspapermen in Paris," he inquired why *they* came here. "On account of the beer," he was told. That word wiped the scowl from his face, momentarily.

LE MONTANA
28 Rue St-Benoît (6e) Tel: 45.48.93.08
Open: weekdays noon to 5 a.m., weekends 6 p.m. to 6 a.m.
Métro: St-Germain-des-Prés

Le Montana, rated in 1988 the best bar in Paris by a local magazine, has long been a private little place just off the Boulevard St-Germain. It is also a jazz club and dining place (offering a 50-franc lunch menu). Above is a hotel by the same name frequented by dozens of writers in this century.

During the postwar decade Sartre used to escape to this bar from the tourists or hangers-on at the Sélect. Beauvoir said they often went for drinks at "the smoking little red inferno of the Montana" with various friends. Filmmakers Goddard, Resnais, Truffaut and Vian argued film philosophy here in the bar.

LA PALETTE
43 Rue de Seine (6e) Tel: 43.26.68.15
Open: 8 a.m. to 1 a.m. (closed Sunday and August)
Métro: Mabillon

La Palette is voted every year the "best outdoor café" in Paris by a local magazine, which notes its ambience, surroundings, the "beer, les Beaux Arts and dependable service with a snarl." Because L'Ecole des Beaux-Arts is just around the corner and up the street, this café has been visited since 1900 by every artist, great or unknown, who has ever sought fame in Paris.

During the first decade of the century, dramatist Alfred Jarry and poets Apollinaire and André Salmon drank absinthe here and engaged in lengthy conversations about literature and aesthetics. They founded a little magazine and would make a profound impact on Surrealism. Later, writers Cyril Connolly, Henry Miller and Jacques Prévert lived up the street in Hôtel La Louisiane (60 Rue Seine) and made a home at La Palette. Sartre and Beauvoir (who also lived at La Louisiane) and their friends ate here often and argued politics during the Algerian war in the 1950s. Beauvoir recalls an epiphany here when talking about a friend who had attempted suicide. While discussing the differences between tranquilizers and antidepressants, she was struck by a sense of her age: "Well that's it, we're on the other side now, we're old." This knowledge hovers over the second volume of her memoirs.

La Palette may have the most beautiful location for a side-walk café in all of Paris. Just north and east of St-Germain-des-Prés, the café guards the corner of a tree-lined square, which is actually a short narrow street (Rue Jacques-Callot) with wide pedestrian walks. On the terrace beneath the trees is plenty of room for sitting on a nice day. There is just enough pedestrian, bicycle and car traffic to keep the scene amusing, but because of the narrow old street, there is enough quiet for hours of relaxation and writing.

Immediately inside the door is a long bar with paint-smeared palettes on the wall above. Coffee at the bar is inexpensive. In this room and the room behind the bar are old mirrors, and the walls and columns are painted with ugly colors that bear the patina of age and make one thirst for a *café-crème*, a color vaguely related to the walls. This was certainly the model for the set of Alan Rudolph's 1988 film, *The Moderns*.

In this district of art schools, galleries and studios, writers and artists have lived for centuries. In the Rue de la Seine, note the plaque of a 17th-century cabaret at No. 26, the building at No. 57 where in 1902 Picasso and a friend took turns sleeping in the only bed, and the Hôtel La Louisiane at No. 60. Almost next door to the Palette is the site of the Surrealist Gallery (No. 16 Rue Jacques-Callot), where American artist Man Ray had his first Dada exhibition; Nancy Cunard's house and Hours Press where she published from 1929–1932 (No. 15 Rue Guénégaud); Rue Mazarine where the French poet Robert Desnos lived for a decade at No. 19; Rue Christine, where Stein and Toklas lived at No. 5; and Rue des Grands-Augustins where, at No. 7, Picasso painted *Guernica*. To the west of Rue de Seine are three historic streets: Rue des Beaux-Arts, where at No. 13 you will find the hotel where Oscar Wilde died in 1900 and where Thomas Wolfe stayed during part of 1925–26, Rue Visconti, where Balzac lived and had a failing printing house at No. 17 and where Jean Racine lived at No. 24, and Rue Jacob, made famous by Natalie Barney, who lived at No. 20 from 1909 to 1973.

LE PETIT ST-BENOÎT
4 Rue St-Benoît (6e) Tel: 42.60.27.92
Open: Monday through Friday, noon to 2:30 p.m., 7 to 10 p.m.
Métro: St-Germain-des-Prés

Le Petit St-Benoît restaurant (called Le Petit Le Varet from 1860 to 1900) has been serving meals to neighbors and literary residents of the dozens of hotels around here for 130 years (the toilet appears to be almost that old!). The place has a tradition, and people dine here who can afford better. Kathryn Hulm remembers in the 1930s a five-franc menu of "whatever was cheapest in Les Halles that day." Marguerite Duras lived across the street during World War II and entertained scores of writers, including François Mitterrand, who came to discuss their resistance work. Maria Jolas dined here with her Joyce crowd after the war (she and her husband Eugene had published James Joyce's *Work in Progress* which later became *Finnegans Wake* in their *transition* magazine before the war). During lunch here shortly after the bombing of Hiroshima, Albert Camus announced to Beauvoir that to prevent atomic war he was "going to ask all scientists in the world to stop their researches." When she suggested that this was "a bit utopian," he flared up. You can see the large, numbered napkin drawers on one wall, used when the clientele were all habitués. The daily mimeographed menu is à la carte and inexpensive; no reservations are taken. You may have to share your table, and your order will be written on the table paper. This is a typical bistro, unlike the instant 1900 look of L'Assiette au Beurre on the corner, which opened only in the 1970s.

BAR DU PONT-ROYAL
7 Rue de Montalembert Tel: 45.44.38.27
Open: noon to midnight (closed Sunday and August)
Métro: Rue du Bac

What the Algonquin on 44th Street in New York City was for American writers, the bar of the Pont-Royal is for French writers. Here in the basement of the Hôtel Pont-Royal, which faces down the Rue du Bac to the Seine, is the little bar of business and post-business drinks for the authors of Editions Gallimard, the major publisher of French literature, located next door in Rue Sébastien-Bottin. For decades, the authors and editors of Gallimard (Editions Nouvelle Revue Française, a monthly review by the same name, and Bibliotheque de La Pléïade) have primed the literary pump here. Gallimard, founded by Jean Schlumberger, Gaston Gallimard and André Gide, has published Proust, Aragon, Simenon, Celine, Cocteau, Gide, Beauvoir, Sartre, Camus and dozens of others, and has pioneered the publication of English literature in translation, from Conrad to Faulkner. Editors and authors adjourn often from the "hutch"—so named because the offices are so small—to the bar.

A seedy old bar down winding stairs, the Pont-Royal suggests the lounge of a ship. It is distinguished by wall panels showing the edict of the king to lay the stone for nearby Pont-Royal (Royal Bridge). Red banquettes and old furniture create a shabby, but comfortably worn, atmosphere. The key to its sustained popularity lies in the privacy it offers its famous customers, who drop in for business as well as for private seductions.

In Beauvoir's memoir, *The Force of Circumstance* (1963), which is punctuated with references to drinks at the Pont-Royal, she recalls eating at Brasserie Lipp on the Boulevard St-Germain, then drinking here until closing time with both Camus and Sartre—the latter on numerous occasions. She and Sartre met Arthur Koestler (*Darkness At Noon*) here one day. He approached their table in the bar and said simply, "Hello. I'm Koestler." When he sat down, according to Beauvoir, he informed Sartre, "You are a better novelist than I am, but not such a good philosopher." Beauvoir thought he was "vain" but "full of warmth," and the three of them spent a great deal of time together here during Koestler's visit.

Next door to the Pont-Royal is the Decameron Bar in the Hôtel Montalembert which catches the literary spillover from Pont-Royal, though it lacks its subterranean privacy. One block the other side of Gallimard is Hôtel Lenox (No. 9 Rue de l'Université), where T. S. Eliot lived in 1910, when he was 22 years old and attending lectures at the Collège de France, and where the James Joyce family lived when they first arrived in Paris in 1920. They were living again in the Lenox when, on Joyce's 40th birthday, 2 February 1922, he received his first copy of *Ulysses* from his publisher, Sylvia Beach.

RESTAURANT DES BEAUX-ARTS
11 Rue Bonaparte (6e) Tel: 43.26.92.64
Open: noon to 2:30 p.m. and 7 to 10:30 p.m.
Métro: St-Germain-des-Prés

Because of its location across from the art school, which has given its name to both the restaurant and the side street, this has been a dining and drinking spot for generations of artists, now chiefly students. It is in almost original condition. Beyond the curved little bar of this bistro, students and workers from nearby galleries and studios crowd around the tables beneath the painted walls and wall paintings. There are three small rooms, two on the ground floor and one on the first floor, each serving a 48-franc menu that includes dessert and wine. For 5 francs more, service included, coffee is served. This is a bargain in any language. Note the bread-cutting box that shows the wear of decades of knives. Oscar Wilde's hotel is just steps down the Rue des Beaux-Arts (look for the ram's head), and the Seine is just a block down Rue Bonaparte.

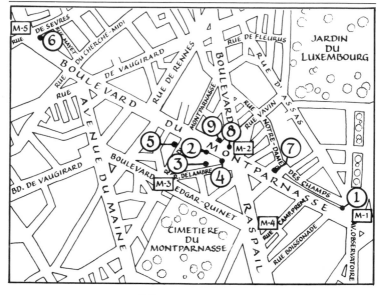

Montparnasse

1. La Closerie des Lilas
2. La Coupole
3. Dingo Bar
4. Café du Dôme
5. Falstaff

6. Café François Coppee
7. Le Jockey
8. La Rotonde
9. Le Sélect

Metro stops:

M-1. Port-Royal
M-2. Vavin
M-3. Edgar Quinet
M-4. Raspail
M-5. Duroc

Cafés of Montparnasse

MONTPARNASSE was once on the outskirts of Paris and had more convents than cafes. Its name came from quarry rubble which University students named after Mount Parnassus, home of the Muses. The quarry was cleared before the 18th century, but the name stuck.

The artists lived and worked north of the river, chiefly in Montmartre, until sometime during the 19th century when they drifted across the river to the Beaux-Arts, Notre-Dame-des-Champs, and the cheap ateliers of the 14th *arrondissement*. This became a region of cafés and cabarets, where the can-can and polka were introduced to Paris. Early in the 20th century, Picasso and his colleagues moved modern art from Montmartre to Montparnasse, and the Dôme and the Sélect became their social center. Before La Coupole opened at the end of 1927, this region between the Luxembourg Gardens and the Montparnasse Cemetery had become a social and literary center of Europe, an international crossroads of art, particularly for "the young degener ation," as one critic observed. One Frenchman called it the "playground for . . . young Yankees." After World War II, Montparnasse was very quiet, but by 1960 it had reestablished its noisy, crowded self.

CLOSERIE DES LILAS
171 Boulevard du Montparnasse (6e) Tel: 43.26.70.50
Open: noon to 1 a.m.
Métro: Port-Royal

The Closerie des Lilas (the lilac arbor) began in the 17th century as a country inn, the first carriage stop on the road from Paris to

Fontainebleu and Orléans. It was frequented from the beginning by the most distinguished poets and artists. Before the Americanization of Montparnasse in the 1920s, when Hemingway wrote "The Big Two-Hearted River" and rewrote *The Sun Also Rises* here, this was the watering hole of the Symbolists, then the Dadaists and Surrealists, and in more recent years Samuel Beckett and many young French poets.

The most famous patrons' names can be found on individual brass markers on the tables inside. In the 19th century, writers Baudelaire, Verlaine, Maeterlinck, Alfred Jarry and Paul Fort, as well as painters, made this their neighborhood café. The art school Académie de la Grande Chaumière was nearby, Whistler's studio was in Rue Notre-Dame-des-Champs, and Cézanne's was in Rue de Chevreuse.

There are many anecdotes of Paul Fort, the "Prince of Poets," as one journalist called him, gathering writers about him each Tuesday evening during the first decade of this century in the room upstairs. Dressed in black from head to toe, the handsome Fort sat on an upholstered bench while poets recited and discussed their poetry. Fort published *Vers et Prose* from 1905 to 1914, and included in its pages the leading Symbolist poets as well as Gide, Apollinaire, Romains and Duhamel, whom he helped discover for the French reading public. Fort wrote his own *Ballades Françaises* as prose lines, not as metric poetry.

After World War I, the Dadaists and Surrealists made this their home, once holding a summit meeting here to determine the ideological purity of certain subscribers to the cause. The meeting disintegrated into chaos. Each generation of writers discovers the Closerie, and the café has undergone both spiritual and physical changes through the years. In *A Moveable Feast*, Hemingway recalls his protests after the renovation of 1923, when the waiters were forced to shave off their mustaches to help attract a wealthier clientele.

Just before Hemingway arrived, James Joyce spent an interesting evening here. Early in February of 1921, he was drinking with a fellow Irishman and expounding on the "superior depth and sonority" of English by quoting passages from the Bible in French and English. "Young man, I say unto thee, arise" is stronger than *"Jeune homme, je te dis, léve-toi,"* he insisted. Joyce was full of language and full of himself, for earlier that day Sylvia Beach had agreed to publish his novel *Ulysses,* upon which he had been laboring for seven years.

Several years later the poetry of the Bible was again read at these tables. Novelist John Dos Passos, who would later write the trilogy *USA,* remembers sitting with Hemingway, drinking vermouth cassis and reading from the Old Testament. "The Song of Deborah and Chronicles and Kings were our favorites." He remembers telling Hemingway to base his sentences on the newspaperman's cable-ese and the King James Bible if he wanted to become the "first great American stylist."

This was Hemingway's neighborhood café when he lived at 113 Rue Notre-Dame-des-Champs (the building he lived in is now gone) from 1924 through the summer of 1926, when he and his first wife Hadley separated. Hemingway fondly describes the café ("my home café") and the statue of Marshall Ney ("my old friend") in his memoirs of his Paris years. He wrote numerous stories here early in the mornings, nursing a *café crème,* occasionally being interrupted by English novelist Ford Madox Ford or the American expatriate poet Ezra Pound who lived in the same street as he (at Numbers 84 and 70). Hemingway also spent time here with F. Scott Fitzgerald, Archibald MacLeish and a dozen other American writers who later penned their memoirs.

Closerie des Lilas has a front open-air terrace for coffee (expensive), a brasserie/café area on the Montparnasse side, a bar area, and a formal restaurant on the Notre-Dame-des-Champs side; the latter is both indoors and outdoors with a retractable roof. If you want a drink at the bar in the evening, find a place near the middle, where the brass plate marked "E. Hemingway" is located, or at a wooden table where the names of famous French patrons are mounted. I do not recommend *Le pavé de rumsteak au poivre*

Hemingway unless you are an incurable romantic. One menu cover quotes Apollinaire, the other quotes Hemingway. The present owners may not understand the rich literary history of the café, but they understand commerce. The bushes, the low awning and the discreet neon signs with their lilac words speak privacy and exclusivity—a century of difference from the original acre of garden where a thousand could dance under the moonlight.

You will find fictional scenes set at the Closerie des Lilas in dozens of works by its patrons, including Hemingway's *The Sun Also Rises* and Thomas Wolfe's *Of Time and the River.*

LA COUPOLE

102 Boulevard du Montparnasse (14e) Tel: 43.20.14.20
Open: every day, 8 a.m. to 2 a.m.
Métro: Vavin

Léon-Paul Fargue said that La Coupole was a "sidewalk academy" where poets and painters learned "bohemian life, scorn for the middle classes, humor and how to hold a glass." Here in the geographic center of Montparnasse, nearly every visiting American writer practiced his lessons. Robert McAlmon, whose writings have been almost forgotten but whose drinking capacity lives on in countless memoirs, often drank here. One cohort said he could drink six whiskeys in thirty minutes "with no apparent effect." McAlmon's Contact Publishing Company issued Hemingway's first book (*Three Stories & Ten Poems*) in 1923. Nevertheless the two men kept up an on-going feud. One night Hemingway approached McAlmon's table and they exchanged insults: "If it isn't Ernest, the fabulous phony! How are the bulls?" taunted McAlmon. "And how is North American McAlmon, the unfinished poem?" Hemingway leaned over and punched McAlmon in the ribs, grinning and "blowing beery breath" over the table.

La Coupole opened its doors on 20 December 1927, on a site that had for years been a coal and lumber yard. This brasserie remained until 1988 the most unchanged of all the Montparnasse literary shrines. Then the Flo business group headed by Jean-Paul Bucher (they own Julien, Boeuf sur le Toit, Flo, and other brasseries) bought the two-story building, the lot to the east and the building to the west. They stored paintings (many of which had disappeared long before), interior columns and other decorative pieces of historical interest, and then demolished the buildings in order to build a higher, more cost-efficient edifice—all with a promise of "restoration" of La Coupole. Initially they set up a public relations office next door to handle the curious and the outraged.

Because La Coupole opened in 1927 as a brasserie, it held the same advantage that Lipp did in St-Germain-des-Prés: it served meals near popular and crowded drinking places (the Sélect and Rotonde are across the street, the Dôme just a few yards up the street). Yet La Coupole offered more: a *café-terrace*, an enormous room for all-day dining and another for dancing in the basement after 4:30. The main floor until 1988 looked like an elegant waiting room in a large railway station, its high ceilings supported by large square columns painted with colorful scenes of café life. The left front entrance originally had a swinging door that opened to a bar. The upstairs was a roof terrace overlooking the boulevard. Later it was roofed in (the rounded roof explained the name) and used for banquets and official dinners. Downstairs, the old marble and wrought-iron tables were replaced by wooden furniture. By 1985 the staff was serving 1,400 meals a day, which included 2,000 oysters.

Little wonder that with its convenience and space it was like a college dining hall for the last years of the raucous 1920s. Memoirs and biographies are full of meetings and parties at La Coupole. American fiction writer Kay Boyle was with McAlmon here one winter night in 1928 when she met Lawrence Vail, the "king of bohemia," whom she married the following year. (Vail would run a commune and art center for decades in Paris.) That same year French poet Louis Aragon first saw French novelist Elsa Triolet here, thus sparking the literary romance of the decade.

In his *Tropic of Cancer*, Henry Miller says that one day, not long after leaving his wife, he was sitting outside at La Coupole "fingering the wedding ring" that he "had tried to pawn off on a *garçon* at the Dôme." The waiter had offered only six francs, and Miller was outraged, "but the belly was getting the upperhand." Hunger and whoring in Paris characterize Miller's *Cancer.* When he could afford to, Miller drank here with his friends, including Lawrence Durrell who had written *The Black Book,* a work steeped in moral decadence. Durrell, who would later earn fame for *The Alexandria Quartet,* claimed he was too poor to eat inside.

> As did every one else [says Durrell], I got drunk at La Coupole when I landed for the first time in Paris. From the terrace, I saw all my heroes passing—I was young. . . . With Anaïs Nin, Miller and [Alfred] Perlès we were the three musketeers of La Coupole. We played chess there. One might say that Perlès almost slept there. . . . As for Anaïs, she quarreled at the bar with her lovers and her publishers. She really liked men, but on all fours, if possible psychiatrists and if possible weeping.

During this time the French, by contrast, were deeply embroiled in political issues. The leading figure of the debates was Ilya Ehrenburg, who hung out at La Coupole, wrote satiric novels, and worked for *Izvestia.* He presided over the Communist corner of the café and was very visible in Montparnasse where, as one critic notes, he had "the leisure to construct a portable, docile USSR, set up in a Paris that he had also built for himself."

Nearly every French and visiting writer of every decade has been seen at one time or another in La Coupole. Samuel Beckett meditated here. Françoise Sagan has often lunched here since writing *Bonjour, tristesse* in 1954 (when she was only twenty). And Gabriel García Márquez, the great Latin American writer (*One Hundred Years of Solitude*) and expatriate, has often dined here.

Dingo Bar (Auberge de Venise)
10 Rue Delambre (14e) Tel: 43.35.43.09
Open: 12:30 to 2:30 p.m., 8 p.m. to midnight
          (closed Sunday and August)
Métro: Vavin or Edgar Quinet

When this was called the Dingo (the Crazy One), it was one of the favorite hangouts of the 1920s. The bar where Hemingway and

Fitzgerald met and where Picasso drank with Jean Cocteau, French poet and collaborator in many art forms, is just inside the front door, and the façade is the same except for the absence of a door, probably removed to make more room for dining. The establishment is now a restaurant, but one may have a drink at the bar.

Legend has it that two visiting English ladies in the 1920s took a taxi to Montparnasse to find the famous night life. As their taxi stopped in front of the Dingo, Florence Martin, an American girl from the Folies Bergère and a regular at all the Montparnasse bars, emerged from the Dingo shouting a string of obscenities. The ladies looked at each other and one said, "This must be the place!" When Jimmy Charters, Dingo's popular English bartender, published his memoirs, he used the line. *This Must Be the Place* (1937) was ghostwritten by Morrill Cody, a regular customer; Hemingway wrote the introduction.

Late in April 1925 Hemingway was drinking here at the bar with an English lady and two other Montparnasse regulars, Duff Twysden and Pat Guthrie, a Scotsman, whom Hemingway would use in his characterizations of Brett Ashley and Mike Campbell in *The Sun Also Rises* the following year. Hemingway was far more interested in the tall, willowy Englishwoman with very short, blond hair than he was in the elegantly-dressed American who approached to introduce himself. Fitzgerald was twenty-eight years old, three years older than Hemingway and a successful novelist. The casually dressed and burly younger man had published a slim collection of short works, but no novels. Fitzgerald ordered champagne and praised the Hemingway stories. The younger writer was embarrassed by public praise, but immediately assumed the superior role. As Matthew Broccoli has argued in his little volume *Scott and Ernest,* Fitzgerald needed a hero to worship and Hemingway needed adulation. The dependency relationship was sealed when Scott turned ashen and nearly passed out from the champagne. Hemingway, who prided himself on always handling his alcohol, was alarmed. Jimmy called a taxi for Fitzgerald.

After 1924 when an American bought the Dingo (founded in

1920), it served corned beef and cabbage, chicken-fried steak and "real American soup." The characters in Hemingway's *The Sun Also Rises* and Harold Loeb's *The Professors Like Vodka* seem to consume only alcohol at the Dingo.

This restaurant just recently became an Italian restaurant, with a colorful new awning outside but the same 1920s bar inside. For eighteen years before this, it was called Auberge du Centre and was owned by Mr. and Mrs. Pierre Berthier, who lived above their restaurant and kept records of its history. They granted photograph and interview sessions at the bar to both Jack Hemingway, Ernest's son, and Scottie Fitzgerald Smith, Scott's daughter.

In the 1920s many American writers, painters and other artists lived and had their studios in this street: Isadora Duncan, Harold Stearns, Man Ray, Jane Heap, John Glassco, Robert McAlmon, Mina Loy, Samuel Putnam and Jo Davidson. Edward Titus operated the Black Manikin Press at No. 4, where he published D. H. Lawrence's *Lady Chatterley's Lover* in 1929.

If you walk down the little Delambre Square and cross Boulevard Edgar Quinet to the cemetery, ask for "Index Sommaire des Célébrités" at the office, and you can locate the grave sites of Tristan Tzara, Baudelaire, Dreyfus and Maupassant. This cemetery contains the remains of many people who lived in and influenced the neighborhood, including Samuel Beckett, Sartre and Beauvoir, the publisher Larousse, the philosopher Edgar Quinet (for whom the boulevard is named), the philanthropist Madame Boucicaut (wife of the founder of the department store Bon Marché in Rue de Sèvres), the sculptor Rude who made the Marshal Ney statue beside the Closerie des Lilas, and the master of literary criticism, Sainte-Beuve.

CAFE DU DÔME

108 Boulevard du Montparnasse (14e) Tel: 43.35.25.81
Open: 10 a.m. to 2 a.m., restaurant opens 12:45 p.m. (closed Monday)
Métro: Vavin or Raspail

What began as a drinking shack at the side of a modest little café in October 1897 has undergone numerous renovations through the years. During World War I its patrons included Lenin, Trotsky, Picasso and Lithuanian painter Chaim Soutine. By the 1920s Americans and Swedes had joined the Russian and Spanish expatriates to make this the major cheap drinking spot on the Left Bank. It was also an informal renting service, loan office, assembly point for parties, place for magazine editors to look for contributors (and vice versa), and zoo for tourists in search of celebrities. It expanded down the street and began offering corn flakes and breakfast. Careers were made and broken at the tables of the

Le Café du Dôme

Dôme, where a boastful Sinclair Lewis, flushed with the success of *Main Street,* was told, "Sit down. You're just a best seller!"

By 1929, according to *The Paris Tribune,* there were fifty books in fifteen languages in which the Café du Dôme figured. The number has multiplied since then and includes the two books that best reflect Paris of the 1920s (*The Sun Also Rises*) and the 1930s (*Tropic of Cancer*). In the latter, Henry Miller presents a surrealistic portrait of Montparnasse at dawn:

> In the blue of an electric dawn the peanut shells look wan and crumpled; along the beach at Montparnasse the water lilies bend and break. When the tide is on the ebb and only a few syphilitic mermaids are left stranded in the muck, the Dôme looks like a shooting gallery that's been struck by a cyclone. Everything is slowly dribbling back to the sewer. For about an hour there is a deathlike calm during which the vomit is mopped up. Suddenly the trees begin to screech. From one end of the boulevard to the other a demented song rises up. It is like the signal that announces the close of the exchange. What hopes there were are swept up. The moment has come to void the last bagful of urine. The day is sneaking in like a leper.

During the 1930s, when Sartre and Beauvoir taught outside Paris, they made the Dôme their Paris base. When Sartre left for the army 2 September 1939, it was the time of morning that Miller writes about. The alarm awakened them at 3 a.m., according to Beauvoir, and they walked to the Dôme in the mild night air. They walked past "two tarts" sitting with their arms around officers on the terrace and entered the noisy and crowded café for coffee, before catching a taxi to the train station.

Since its latest renovation in 1986, the Dôme has become one of the best fish restaurants on the Left Bank, also selling fresh fish from the shop around the corner. The bouillabaisse for two is a meal in itself. Slavik (who designed the first Paris drugstores) decorated the interior, which features dark wood, mirrors and brass, and lights softened by peach-colored gauze. Toward the right are brass plaques with the names of former customers below several pictures of each: Braque, Derain, Zadkine, Kisling, Foujita,

Modigliani and other great painters of the first half of this century. Scattered throughout the restaurant are also pictures of famous writers and celebrities who have frequented the café—including Sartre, Beauvoir and Beckett.

FALSTAFF

42 Rue du Montparnasse (14e) Tel: 43.35.38.29
Open: 7 p.m. to 11:30 p.m. (closed July)
Métro: Edgar Quinet

Just off the boulevard is an English bar that has like the Dingo been a favorite drinking place for those who wished to avoid the large, crowded and bright cafés of the boulevard. In the late 1920s the stuffy oak paneling, padded seats, huge copper machine for draft beer and English atmosphere contrasted to the easy and haphazard ambience set by the barman, Jimmy Charters. When Jimmy moved to the Falstaff from the Dingo, he made this a popular café for Americans and English.

Morley Callaghan, one of Canada's best short story writers, drank here with Hemingway, Fitzgerald and McAlmon. Callaghan remembers coming here after boxing matches with Hemingway. They liked to talk with Jimmy, who had been a prizefighter in England.

Another Canadian, John Glassco, was in the Falstaff in 1928 when the galley sheets of Djuna Barnes's *Ladies Almanack* were passed around. He describes the scene as rather glum, though the book is a lusty celebration of lesbian love in the 17th and 18th centuries, with fictional characters representing a number of the contemporary lesbians of the quarter. Barnes was a hard-drinking Irish-American whom many considered a serious and promising writer. Her reputation, particularly for *Nightwood*, has grown through the years.

A number of French writers mention eating at the Falstaff as well. On the second floor, Jean-Paul Sartre gave a preopening supper for the company of his play, *The Condemned of Altona*, in 1956 before flying off to Ireland to confer with John Huston on a film script. In torment over having to make cuts in the play, though he did so later, he drank a great deal. When the play opened, the critics agreed that it was his best.

This street, which runs just a block on each side of the boulevard, has several important addresses, including the home of Sainte-Beuve, the French poet and literary critic, at No. 11, and Larousse publishers at No. 13 and No. 17.

CAFE FRANÇOIS COPPÉE

1 bis Boulevard du Montparnasse (6e) Tel: 47.34.72.70
Open: 7 a.m. to 9 p.m. (closed Sunday and August)
Métro: Duroc

The Boulevard du Montparnasse is framed by this café at No. 1 bis and by Closerie des Lilas at No. 171. Between them lie the Dôme, Rotonde, Coupole, Sélect, Falstaff, Dingo, Jockey and less known hangouts. The Coppée, still a lively but ordinary café, merits our attention because of two French poets who are closely associated with it.

François Coppée, who wrote delicate and sentimental French verse in the latter 19th century, was a devoté of this café—then called Café des Vosges. He lived a couple of blocks away in Rue Oudinot and met his friends here at the end of the day. He had his own table, as people usually did, and gathered many about him because he was quite a talker. When he died, the owner rechristened his café after his faithful customer. For a long time it was humorously called "des Vosges et de François Coppée," now simply Le François Coppée. The café was destroyed and rebuilt when the building was replaced in 1934.

Later in his life, Léon-Paul Fargue lived at the top of this new building (note the plaque), where he died in 1947 at the age of seventy-one. Fargue was a devoted friend of Marie Monnier and her sister Adrienne, owner of La Maison des Amis des Livres at 7 Rue de l'Odéon. He had a reputation in his early years for visiting friends in the middle of the night during prowlings of the city he loved and celebrated in his poetry. He was always fond of crowded cafés, especially the François Coppée, where he could move from table to table, friend to friend, conversation to conversation. He talked out many a poem and book at his table here. Actually, he talked, and a friend wrote down his words. When the sun was bright, he would sit under the awning and "fancy" himself "at Deauville," a resort on the Normandy coast. Because he had a stroke (from which he recovered) during World War II when elevators were not in use, he hired two strong men to hoist him with ropes and pulleys on a chair "up and down the goods-lift." Once on the street he walked into the crowded café. Occasionally he would sleep an hour or two at his table—he called it "taking a dip."

The terrace of the Coppée forms the corner of the Boulevard du Montparnasse, where it joins Boulevard des Invalides and Rue de Sèvres. Like Deux-Magots and Dôme, the Coppée overlooks a major intersection just steps from a métro stop. During wet or cold weather, the glass-enclosed area protects the visitor, who can look out onto the intersection of three arrondissements: the old sixth, which includes part of the Latin Quarter, the elegant seventh of the Eiffel Tower and Invalides (Napoleon's Tomb), and across the boulevard to the fifteenth, where many painters and sculptors had their studios. Parallel to Rue de Sèvres is Rue du Cherche-Midi, well known for its good restaurants and Poilâne bread bakery (at No. 8). If you wish to visit the Rodin Museum, walk down the Boulevard des Invalides to Rue de Varenne.

LE JOCKEY
127 Boulevard du Montparnasse (6e) Tel: 43.20.63.02
Open: 9 a.m. to 2 a.m.
Métro: Vavin

The second site of the Jockey, called Le Congrès since 1991, bears little resemblance to the original cabaret. The club was first located up the street at No. 146 (at the corner of Rue Campagne Première) and began with the name Académie du Caméléon, a literary and artistic cabaret that operated from March 1921 to November 1923. It was renamed by the new owner, "Jockey" Miller, and then taken over by Hilaire Hiler, an American painter who often played the piano. Kiki, the model and mistress of many, sang torch songs and passed the hat. The cabaret moved across the street to the corner of Rue du

Chevreuse and apparently continued to operate until the Second World War. It has been a restaurant for several years, with only a recent name change.

The Jockey that packed them in during the 1920s at both locations on the boulevard was decorated inside and out with large painted figures that covered each one-story building. Old pictures show a painting of an Indian riding an Appaloosa near the entrance of both buildings. Inside the place that Hemingway called the best nightclub "that ever was," people were packed like sardines around a tiny floor space. Cocteau, Duchamp and Louis Aragon were regulars. The bartender was an American Indian who had stayed in Paris after Buffalo Bill's Wild West Show took the city by storm in the spring of 1905. Kiki sang her songs with suggestive gestures and exposed white thighs that contrasted to her black hair and dress. She initiated an unknown number of eager youths, but lived for many years with Man Ray, American surrealist painter and photographer.

LA ROTONDE

105 Boulevard du Montparnasse (6e) Tel: 43.26.68.84
Open: 8 a.m. to 2 a.m.
Métro: Vavin

Legend has it that the shift from the Rotonde to the Dôme occurred one day when the manager of the Rotonde refused to serve a young woman who was sitting at this *café-terrasse* without a hat (gasp!) and smoking a cigarette. When she walked defiantly across the boulevard, the Dôme manager tipped the tide of history with his leniency. Whether the story is true or not, many patrons of the 1920s, including Malcolm Cowley and Peggy Guggenheim, record that they and their friends denounced the intolerance of the Rotonde and quarreled with the owner. On Bastille Day 1923, Louis Aragon, Lawrence Vail and Malcolm Cowley were sitting at the Dôme discussing the rudeness of the owner of the Rotonde and the possibility that he was a police informer who had betrayed several anarchists. They crossed the street and made loud demands; finally Cowley took a swing at the *patron*, catching him in the jaw—a blow that ensured Cowley's immortality in the history of Dada. But the incident got him arrested in the street later, after they had fled the Rotonde. Friends insisted that he was not in the café, which gave him time to catch his ship home. His *Exile's Return* is one of the best assessments of the 1920s.

The café, which opened in 1911—three years after Simone de Beauvoir was born upstairs in this building—served more serious revolutionaries than the naughty Dadaists. It attracted Lenin, Trotsky and other political exiles in the days when Paris was a refuge for Russian conspirators of the old school. Then it attracted an international group of painters, including Picasso, Derain, Vlaminck, Salmon, Max Jacob, Modigliani and Kisling. About 1923 or 1924, the Rotonde expanded by taking over the Café du Parnasse at No. 103 and brought in the middle class with a grill room, café-terrasse, dance hall upstairs and night bar. Some of the old habitués no longer felt at home, as the Cowley incident illustrates. Hemingway criticized the "scum" of the Rotonde with their "careless individuality" when he first came to Paris in December 1921 and was writing pieces for the *Toronto Star Weekly*. Pretty soon he himself was cultivating the long-haired, shabby look, and by the time he wrote *The Sun Also Rises* he was a regular. His Jake Barnes says that "no matter what café in Montparnasse you ask a taxi driver to bring you to from the right bank of the river, they always take you to the Rotonde." The poet or painter who wanted "to succeed in Bucharest or in Seville must necessarily," said Fargue, "... do a tour of duty at the Rotonde or the Coupole."

By the late 1950s the Rotonde was taken over in part (the No. 103 address) by a cinema, and today the original site sports the red-plush 1900 look that is so popular. Yet the location will always keep it attractive, for unlike terraces at the Dôme and the Coupole, the one at the Rotonde catches the best sun. This sun-baked terrace covers the corner between the métro stop Vavin and Rodin's statue of Balzac in the Boulevard Raspail.

LE SÉLECT
99 Boulevard du Montparnasse (6e) Tel: 45.48.38.24
Open: 8 a.m. to 3 a.m.
Métro: Vavin

Café Le Sélect opened in 1925 to immediate popularity: it was the first Montparnasse establishment to remain open all night and to gather at dawn the last night owls of the quarter. It was very popular, especially for its chess games, with the White Russian refugees, who added much color to the Montparnasse scene between the wars. It remains a comfortable, homey café, relatively unchanged, with tan walls, red banquettes, and a skylight of glass brick in the back to aid master chess players. Coffee at the bar is reasonably priced. So far it has escaped the instant Art Deco or Art Nouveau style, unlike the Rotonde, which has succumbed to garish red plush, and the Dôme, full of filmy peach. This is the real thing. It also serves one of the best sandwiches in the quarter, the Croque Sélect.

The Sélect's best known patron in its early years was Harold Stearns, who personified the critics' view of the "lost" of his generation. Stearns was a respected writer and social critic when he came in 1921 from Massachusetts (via Greenwich Village) to Paris, where he almost disappeared into a bottle. Hemingway and others often found him drinking at the bar, unshaven, a pile of saucers in front of him. He appears thus as Harvey Stone in *The Sun Also Rises*, where Jake, as did Hemingway in real life, gives him some money for food. Stearns spent his time drinking in the cafés or at the race tracks where, to support himself, he reported for the Paris *Chicago Tribune* under the name "Peter Pickem." He also appears as Wiltshire Tobin in Kay Boyle's novel *Monday Night*. Stearns lived in the hotel next door in Rue Vavin (No. 50), where Louise Bryant was living when she died. Bryant was the widow of John Reed (their story is told in the film *Reds*) and former wife of William Bullitt, the U.S. Ambassador to France.

In the Sélect, American dancer Isadora Duncan got into a violent discussion about the Sacco and Vanzetti case with Floyd

Gibbons, a war correspondent for the *Chicago Tribune* who had lost an eye at Château-Thierry and wore a black patch. When Gibbons claimed that the Italian anarchists were given a "fair trial," Duncan became furious and gave Gibbons a "tongue-lashing," according to one observer. Soon there were sympathizers on both sides, and the yelling turned to glass throwing. The police intervened, but Duncan would not calm down because Sacco and Vanzetti were scheduled to be executed in Boston that very evening. It was beginning to rain, but she took her followers and marched down the Boulevard Raspail and on for two miles to the American Embassy across the river. There outside the locked gates, guarded by a platoon of steel-helmeted gendarmes, she held high a burning taper and kept a silent vigil in the chill drizzle for the rest of the night. At dawn an American reporter arrived and informed her that the executions had again been delayed. "Thank God!" she sighed and quietly left. Later when Sacco and Vanzetti were indeed put to death, rioting broke out around Paris and French crowds invaded the cafés where Americans drank to protest.

But the most famous fight in the Sélect was initiated by the inebriated Hart Crane, who could not stay away from the bottle. After a nasty argument with a waiter, and then with Madame Sélect, who was not tolerant of loud Americans, Crane was ushered out by the police. When he took a swing at them, the police beat him unconscious and took him to jail, where he remained for a week. Maria Jolas heard about his arrest and told Harry and Caresse Crosby, who were preparing to publish Crane's *The Bridge* at their Black Sun Press. The Crosbys, Kay Boyle and Lawrence Vail rallied support and funds for his release. Not long after this, on 18 July 1929, Crane was on the ship home. The following year *The Bridge* appeared, just weeks after Harry Crosby's suicide in New York. Crane took his life less than three years later by jumping from the stern of a steamship returning from Mexico to New York.

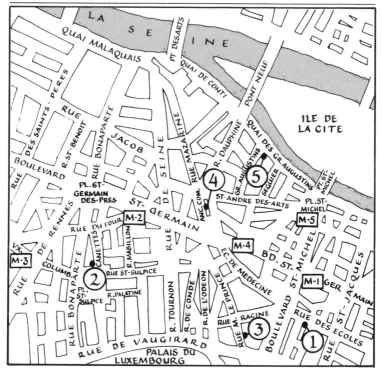

The Latin Quarter

1. Brasserie Balzar
2. Café de la Mairie
3. Crémerie Restaurant Polidor
4. Le Procope
5. Lapérouse

Metro stops:

M-1. Cluny
M-2. Mabillon
M-3. St-Sulpice
M-4. Odéon
M-5. St-Michel

Cafés of the Latin Quarter

A MONG THE following five cafés that fan out around the
Carrefour de l'Odéon is the oldest café in Paris, the Procope,
founded in 1686. A century or two ago there were many other
venerable and influential literary cafés in this region from Foyot at
the intersection of Rue de Vaugirard and Rue de Tournon east to
La Pomme-de-Pin (the Pine Cone) in Place de la Contrescarpe, a
café described by Rabelais and where in the early 1550s seven poets
founded the Pléiade Society to encourage writing in French, as
against Latin. Until 1956 Café Voltaire served in Place de l'Odéon,
hosting the Encyclopédists (Rousseau, Voltaire, Diderot) in the
mid-18th century, Rodin, Verlaine, Mallarmé and Gauguin in the
19th century, and then Valéry, Gide, and Sartre, as well as the
editors of Mercure de France, the publishing house around the
corner. Café d'Harcourt and Café François Premier, both favorites
of the Symbolists, are long gone from Boulevard Saint-Michel, as
is the Taverne du Panthéon, where at a "dinner of the Argonauts,"
Jerry shoots himself in André Gide's *The Counterfeiters*.

Fortunately, three of the old café-restaurants are active today:
Procope, founded in the mid-17th century, and Polidor and
Lapérouse, founded in the mid-18th century. The Procope has
changed the most, catering more to tourists now, and the Polidor
the least, still serving poor students at long tables. Lapérouse
periodically regilds its gold leaf for well-to-do clients.

BRASSERIE BALZAR

49 Rue des Ecoles (5e) Tel: 43.54.25.73
Open: 8 a.m. to 1 a.m.
Métro: Cluny

Opened in the 1890s, this Alsatian brasserie shares with Brasserie Lipp the distinction of being one of the best brasseries on the Left Bank. Many people prefer the food at Balzar over Lipp's. Warren Trabant, an American expatriate in Paris who writes about food, recommends the pigs' feet "Sainte-Menehould." Lipp owned this café for a number of years beginning in the early 1930s. Because it is around the corner from the Sorbonne, the University of Paris has influenced the *mise en scène*. People from the theater, writers, playwrights, and above all professors have always eaten here.

In his *20th Century Journey,* newspaperman William L. Shirer describes walking from the Rue La Fayette on the Right Bank to this brasserie. It was in the middle of the night after he had finished his first night on the job, putting the *Chicago Tribune* to bed in 1925. With his fellow workers Eugene Jolas, Elliot Paul and James Thurber, he walked down to the Halles, through the Place du Châtelet, across Ile de la Cité to the brightly lighted Brasserie Balzar, where they "downed a few beers and a plate of sauerkraut and sausage" before going home to bed. There was "a cluster of professors having a nightcap" nearby and former Premier Edouard Herriot at another table. Shirer, Paul and Thurber made this their regular eating place because most of them lived nearby. Elliot Paul lived in Rue de la Huchette, which he immortalized in *The Last Time I Saw Paris* and *Springtime in Paris.*

From the Brasserie Balzar one can visit the Sorbonne, around the corner to the right, or the Musée de Cluny, across the street and around the corner.

CAFÉ DE LA MAIRIE

8 Place St-Sulpice (6e) Tel: 43.26.67.82
Open: 8 a.m. to 1 or 2 a.m.
Métro: Mabillon or St-Sulpice

Since the middle of the 1920s this has been a favorite café of writers, on a square beloved by Anatole France and designed for solitude, tucked away as it is from noisy St-Germain-des-Prés. Hemingway describes the fountain in the "quiet square" and the pigeons "perched on the statues of the bishops" (*A Moveable Feast*). A hungry Henry Miller curses the pigeons for making the crumbs disappear like magic (*Tropic of Cancer*). They both drank at this café, as did Djuna Barnes, who set her novel *Nightwood* here and in the Hôtel Récamier across the square. Beckett breakfasted here. Simone de Beauvoir saw Camus here for the last time with Sartre, before the two men quarreled in 1951. And Saul Bellow says he never goes to the Deux-Magots or Flore, but prefers this quiet café on St-Sulpice.

Among the many writers who lived nearby were Faulkner (26 Rue Servandoni), Hemingway (6 Rue Férou) and Fitzgerald (somewhere in Rue de Mézières). The latter set the story "Babylon Revisited" in Rue Palatine. In the 19th century, before these moderns haunted the streets, this territory between Place St-Sulpice and the Luxembourg Gardens belonged to Alexandre Dumas and his Three Musketeers: Aramis lived just east of Rue Cassette, Athos lived in Rue Férou, Porthos had his pretended residence in Rue du Vieux-Colombier, and D'Artagnan's first home was in Rue des Fossoyeurs (now Rue Servandoni).

Le Café de la Mairie

While you are in the neighborhood, visit the Village Voice Bookstore in the Rue Princesse and the Church of St-Sulpice (1749), especially the Chapel of the Virgin Mary behind the high altar, where Hemingway claims to have lighted a candle after he had trouble in bed with his second wife Pauline. He told A. E. Hotchner that he successfully tested the candle immediately after they returned to their Rue Férou apartment. Young Scottie Fitzgerald attended Mass here, as did Faulkner. "Be a good Catholic soon," Faulkner wrote his mother. He spent every day of his summer and fall (1925) in Paris sitting in the Luxembourg Gardens, which is only a block away.

CRÉMERIE RESTAURANT POLIDOR

41 Rue Monsieur-le-Prince (6e) Tel: 43.26.95.34
Open: 12:30 to 2:30 p.m., 7:30 p.m. to 1 a.m.
    (closes 10 p.m. Sunday)
Métro: Odéon

In 1902–1903, when an Irish lad named James Joyce lived around the corner and beside the theater in Rue Corneille, he ate here when he could—that is, when money orders arrived from Dublin. He was writing literary reviews, reading in the libraries, and creating his theories of art while he cultivated a bohemian appearance and attitude. He ate from a menu that featured BOF (butter, eggs and cheese). Crémeries, which flourished in the Latin Quarter for students of the bohemian class, served simple, fresh meals and large bowls of coffee or chocolate or boiled milk with rice for a few pennies.

This crémerie opened in 1845 and by 1890 was a real restaurant, or rather a *bistro* or *bouillon,* which better suits this dining room with its long tables and inexpensive food. It is located near the Sorbonne and numerous bookshops and publishing companies, and it attracts students and visitors from many countries (one column of the menu is in English). The menu is long and features simple food.

The list of great patrons is as long as the menu and includes Rimbaud and Verlaine in the 19th century as well as Joyce early in this century and later American novelist Richard Wright. The Collège de Pataphysique (Science of Improbables) meets in the Polidor. These disciples of Alfred Jarry once included poet/painter Max Ernst, playwright Eugène Ionesco and film director René Clair. The present day absurdists or surrealists continue their playful gatherings. The Friends of Paul Verlaine also hold their occasional meetings at the Polidor.

Fortunately for poor students and professors, the Polidor has thus far resisted the trend to tart up the establishment—you can still eat on ancient tiles beside simple antique mirrors. When you leave the restaurant, turn left to find the Place de la Sorbonne or the Place du Panthéon. Turn right and then left to reach the Odéon Theater. Richard Wright lived at No. 14 Rue Monsieur-le-Prince from 1948 until his death in 1960, where he wrote an autobiography and several novels (including *Black Boy*) and, in March 1959, entertained Martin Luther King, Jr.

LE PROCOPE

13 Rue de l'Ancienne-Comédie (6e) Tel: 43.26.99.20
Open: everyday from 8 a.m. to 2 p.m.
Métro: Odéon

When Benjamin Franklin died in 1790 and the French Assembly went into mourning for three days, the Procope was draped in black in honor of one of its patrons and France's favorite American.

The café, which opened here in 1686 (presumably it first opened in 1675 in Rue de Tournon), was the birthplace in the 18th century of the rationalist *Encyclopédie*, conceived during a conversation between Diderot and d'Alembert. These men, as well as Voltaire (perhaps Procope's patron saint), Rousseau and Beaumarchais met here frequently. On the evening of 27 April 1784, Beaumarchais sat here at a table while his *Marriage of Figaro* opened nearby at the Odéon Theater. Danton and Marat met here during the Revolution; find the statue of Danton nearby in the Boulevard Saint Germain, facing the street named after him. These Frenchmen along with Benjamin Franklin, Thomas

...on and John Paul Jones helped to make this the most famous Parisian café in the 18th century. Though it is the oldest café in Paris, it is no longer famous for its food or for its illustrious patrons.

The café received its name from its founder, Francesco Procopio dei Coltelli, a Sicilian nobleman who had the foresight to anticipate the appeal of coffee at a time when it was just a novelty. Of course, he was Italian! Coffee and the popularity of the Comédie-Française, which opened across the street in 1689, ensured the café's success. In the 19th century it was patronized by Hugo, Musset, George Sand, Balzac, Gautier, Verlaine, then Zola, Huysmans, Maupassant and Cézanne. It bills itself as *Le Rendezvous des Arts et des Lettres.*

When the Procope opened its doors on 14 June 1988 after a complete renovation, it was full of reminders of its coffeehouse origins: black bartenders (coffee servers) in red fez, coffee tables with newspapers (including the *Herald Tribune*) just inside the door, a glass display case with artifacts of coffeehouses, and waiters in period suits of white blouses, gray sleeveless jackets and black baggy pants. Yet the computerized ordering system (each waiter has a plastic card) and the show tunes on the player piano jar the historic atmosphere. It all looks like a fake 18th-century living room. The red and gold seem garish under the bright lights, but remember that Emerson found the cafés "blazing with light" during his visit to Paris in the early 19th century. The visiting clientele today seem happy—and the large chrome and marble oyster bar promises fresh fish.

When leaving the restaurant, note the plaque across the street commemorating the original Comédie-Française. If you turn right and go around the corner to the Rue St-André-des-Arts (every street is rich with literary associations), you will find No. 46, where E. E. Cummings lived in 1923 during one of his many trips to Paris, which he celebrated in his poetry; No. 41, where Racine lived from 1680 to 1684; No. 28, where Jack Kerouac, in 1962, drank at what he called "the perfect bar", La Gentilhommière (now gone); and No. 25, where in the basement Baudelaire drank at an ancient cabaret.

LAPÉROUSE

51 Quai des Grands-Augustins (6e) Tel: 43.26.68.04
Open: 12:30 to 2:30 p.m., 8 to midnight
        (closed Sunday evening and Monday)
Métro: Saint-Michel

If you want to see what a good restaurant of 150 years ago looked like, go to Lapérouse. After dark chandeliers illuminate the two upper floors which are honey-combed with private rooms. The river bank affords an excellent view of this attractive spectacle. Precisely when this restaurant facing the Seine was founded is uncertain, but it was sometime after the middle of the 19th century. It had a star in the 1888 Baedeker and was on the same footing as Tour d'Argent and Foyot in the 1890's. It is an authentic Belle Epoque landmark, decorated with dark wood, gilded trim, old paintings of peasants and country scenes, small balconies of Louis XV grillwork and lots of patina.

Originally it was a more modest restaurant where Jules Lefèvre, a wine merchant, catered to the merchants of the nearby Market of the Valley, which specialized in poultry and game. He opened the first upper floor for these merchants and their attorneys and agents to conduct business—hence the private dining rooms today. When the market moved, the restaurant did not die, but attracted editors and writers. Maupassant, Hugo, Dumas, Thackeray and Robert Louis Stevenson enjoyed Lapérouse. This probably is the restaurant where Lambert Strether dines on several occasions in Henry James's *The Ambassadors*. In later years Proust and Colette dined here. Senators and businessmen, it is said, once used the small rooms for assignations.

Lapérouse is very expensive, but the 18th-century mansion is a work of art and the location is grand. Directly across the river in the Ile de la Cité is Restaurant Paul, probably the prototype of Brasserie Dauphine of the novels of Georges Simenon—the café which, since 1929, Inspector Maigret has frequented.

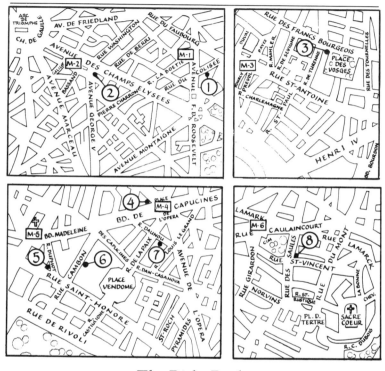

The Right Bank

1. Le Boeuf súr le Toit
2. Le Fouquet's
3. Ma Bourgogne
4. Café de la Paix
5. Prunier
6. Hemingway Bar (Hôtel Ritz)
7. Harry's New York Bar
8. Le Lapin Agile

Metro stops:

M-1. St-Philippe-du-Roule
M-2. George V
M-3. St. Paul
M-4. Opéra
M-5. Madeleine
M-6. Lamarck Caulaincourt

Right Bank Cafés and Restaurants

BEFORE the 20th century, artists usually lived on the Right Bank of the Seine, which includes the low-rent Montmartre quarter. With few exceptions, the grand old cafés of the previous century were located on the Right Bank. Most of them have disappeared: Durand in the Place de la Madeleine, where Zola wrote "J'accuse"; La Régence across from the Comédie-Française, where Bonaparte played chess; Café des Milles Colonnes in the Palais-Royal, where Sir Walter Scott dined; and Café Anglais on the Boulevard des Italiens, where the elder Dumas wrote his weekly installment of *Les Trois Mousquetaires*.

Two 19th-century cafés remain today: Fouquet's on Avenue des Champs Elysées, and Café de la Paix on Boulevard des Capucines and Place de l'Opéra. Of the three other literary cafés or restaurants mentioned below, Prunier deliberately cultivated American writers and journalists, and Le Boeuf sur le Toit was a cabaret founded by artists. Ma Bourgogne, Fouquet's and Café de la Paix have sidewalk terraces for drinking. Le Boeuf sur le Toit and Prunier are restaurants with indoor bars.

LE BOEUF SUR LE TOIT
34 Rue du Colisée (8e) Tel: 43.59.83.80
Open: noon to 2 a.m.
Métro: St-Philippe-du-Roule

Here just off the Avenue Franklin-Roosevelt is the fourth location in the 8th *arrondissement* of the Ox on the Roof. It began in Rue Duphot, moved to 28 Rue Boissy-d'Anglas, where it enjoyed its greatest period of fame, then moved to larger quarters at 26 Rue de

Penthièvre, at Rue du Faubourg St-Honoré. The present location, a creation of the Flo brasserie group, is on a street that ends at Rue du Faubourg St-Honoré.

The Dadaist-sounding name originated right after the First World War, when Paul Claudel told Jean Cocteau he had seen this name on an inn in Brazil. Cocteau used the name for a new ballet-pantomime, which he created with the collaboration of Darius Milhaud and the Fratellini brothers in 1920. He also gave the name to Louis Moysès, who had just opened a bar which they and Milhaud publicized as a cabaret for musicians and composers. Cocteau, who reigned from midnight to dawn, called it "un rendez-vous de chasse spirituel." Fargue called it "a sort of society *Académie*," and Paul Valéry said it was the place where art met music, which met society, which met politics, which met money, which met literature, which in turn met smart bohemianism, and so on till the circle was complete.

The second home of this *monument poétique* is gone, but the present incarnation is dedicated to its memory and serves as a great stage set for the 1930s. The outside, with its curved windows and art deco signs, the piano bar, and the careful detail of the decor are far more lavish than any of the many earlier incarnations of Le

Le Boeuf sur le Toit

Boeuf. Beyond the large fresh-fish store/oyster bar is a display case of photographs and memorabilia of the previous Le Boeufs. Lunch and dinner are expensive.

LE FOUQUET'S

99 Avenue des Champs Elysées (8e) Tel: 47.23.70.60
Open: 9 a.m. to 3 a.m.
Métro: George V

"We dine in Fouquet's very frequently, in fact almost always," James Joyce wrote to his son and daughter-in-law on 1 July 1934. "It has become a chic prize-ring. The other night an advanced lady slapped a perfect gentleman's face on account of another perfect lady's being with him." He continues narrating further slaps and scuffles, concluding that "some people are so playful." The Joyces ate and drank here regularly during the 1930s when they lived a few blocks away at 42 Rue Galilee and later just across the Seine at 7 Rue Edmond Valentin. Joyce enjoyed elegant surroundings and preferred white wine (lightning, he called it) to red (beef-steak, he said). According to the French critic and editor Louis Gillet, Joyce sat at the same table and in the same seat and ordered the same menu (marenne oysters, chicken, flap mushrooms or asparagus, cup of fruit or ice-cream), though he never touched the food; he smoked and emptied three or four carafes of Muscadet before midnight. Joyce, a "man of habit," listened absentmindedly to his guests' conversation and lapsed into frequent silences, according to Gillet. During this decade of dining at Fouquet's, Joyce was working on his last novel, *Finnegans Wake*, suffering from nerves and poor health (he died of a perforated duodenal ulcer in 1941), and struggling to save his mentally ill daughter, Lucia.

Le Fouquet's, the most popular Right Bank café, was founded in 1899 as an Alsatian café and restaurant. It was threatened with closure in the summer of 1988 when new owners of the building raised their heretofore meager rent ninefold. Front-page news articles, preservation committees and petitions finally moved the French Cultural Minister to announce in October the café-restaurant's continuance as a cultural monument. A major setting for society news, Fouguet's attracts film directors (Algerian Lakhdar Hamina uses the café for his headquarters), film stars, journalists and establishment writers.

Located on the busy intersections of Avenues George V and Champs-Elysées, Fouguet's (pronounce the "t" as in "bets") is famous for its bar, which is on the ground floor in the café. Fouguet's Elysées Restaurant (closed July 15 to September 1, and weekends) is upstairs on the first floor. You may wish to see the brass plaques naming famous patrons now dead, and the silver napkin rings saved for the famous regulars (still living).

MA BOURGOGNE

19 Place des Vosges (4e) Tel: 42.78.44.64
Open: 8 a.m. to 11:30 p.m. (closed Monday)
Métro: St-Paul

Here at the corner of Place des Vosges, one of the oldest squares in Paris, and Rue des Francs Bourgeois is the best and busiest café in the Marais—the quarter where from the 15th to the 18th centuries the aristocracy of Paris lived. Hôtel des Tournelles dates from about 1400, and the plaza was completed early in the 17th century.

Here under the historic arches you can have a drink with local residents and the 17th-century ghosts of those who dueled in the square. You will be drinking also with Inspector Maigret of Georges Simenon's detective stories, who stops here regularly.

A café has been at this location at least since the turn of the century, and Ma Bourgogne herself has been presiding here since World War II. About 1960 Sartre and Beauvoir took refuge in this café after being nearly crushed in a political demonstration at the St-Paul métro stop. They had tried to catch a train following a demonstration and tear-gassing in the Place de la Bastille against De Gaulle's actions in Algeria.

In the Place des Vosges lived Cardinal Richelieu at No. 21, Theophile Gautier at No. 8, and Victor Hugo at No. 6. The latter building was used by Dumas as home of the sinister Mylady of *The Three Musketeers* and is now the Hugo Museum, open 10 a.m. to

5:50 p.m. (closed Monday and Tuesday). Outside the northeast corner of the square at Nos. 30–36 Rue des Tournelles was the great 17th-century literary salon of Ninon de Lenclos, who entertained La Fontaine, Boileau, La Rochefoucauld, and Molière, who read *Tartuffe* aloud here. Out the northwest side of the square you can find the Picasso Museum at 5 Rue de Thorigny, open 10 a.m. to 5 p.m. (10 p.m. Wednesday), closed Tuesday.

CAFÉ DE LA PAIX

5 Place de l'Opéra (9e) Tel: 42.68.12.12
Open: 10 a.m. to 1:30 a.m.
    (restaurant closed in August)
Métro: Opéra

An historical monument to the Belle Epoque, Café de la Paix was founded at the same time as the Paris Opéra in 1872. Its marble pillars, ornate façade, and trompe l'oeil of skies and cherubs on the gold ceiling represented the height of Victorian architecture. This is the last of the grand cafés, which once included (on the Boulevard des Italiens, approaching from the Café de la Paix), Café de Paris at No. 24, Tortoni's at No. 22, Maison Dorée at No. 20, Café Riche at No. 16, Café Anglais at No. 13. As Balzac, Flaubert, Maupassant and Henry James illustrate in their fiction, this was the center of 19th-century Parisian life—the "center of the civilized world."

Clients of La Paix have included poets and film stars, kings and princes. James met Turgenev here (or in a room above in the Grand Hôtel). Foreign newsmen who worked nearby including Booth Tarkington, John Dos Passos and Gilbert Seldes—drank here. George Gurdjieff, the Russo-Greek mystic, had a regular breakfast table in the café, where he met his followers, who included A. R. Orage (*New Age*), Margaret Anderson, Solita Solano, Georgette Leblanc and Kathryn Hulme. At the liberation of Paris in August of 1944, De Gaulle ate here before his famous walk from the Etoile down the Champs Elysées. He ordered an omelette.

Not surprisingly, the café and the Grand Hôtel appear in numerous novels and short stories, including Zola's *Nana*, Henry

James's *The American,* Booth Tarkington's *The Beautiful Lady,* Richard Harding Davis's *The Princess Aline,* Thomas Wolfe's *Of Time and the River,* and Hemingway's "My Old Man" and *The Sun Also Rises.*

PRUNIER
9 Rue Duphot (1e) Tel: 42.60.36.04
Open: 12:30 to 2:30 p.m., 7:30 to 10:30 p.m.
Métro: Madeleine

Zelda and F. Scott Fitzgerald always ordered Pouilly and bouillabaisse when they ate here in the 1920s. Hadley and Ernest Hemingway celebrated here after winning at the races; they had oysters and *crabe mexicain* with glasses of Sancerre. After World War II, Hemingway and his fourth wife, Mary, dined here with Marlene Dietrich. Mary remembered two bottles of Sancerre.

Prunier restaurant—there is a branch now on Avenue des Champs-Elysées—began as an oyster shop in 1872, patronized mainly by Americans and British. The story goes that cooking began when a Bostonian asked Emile Prunier to cook his oysters, then had to demonstrate the procedure in Prunier's kitchen. Prunier, who planted beds of Cape Cod clams and Blue Point oysters in Brittany, took out generous advertising space in the Paris *Herald.* Many young American writers who supported themselves first as journalists enjoyed the seafood here.

One can eat inside downstairs or outside from the oyster bar, or dine upstairs à la carte. There are private rooms and a piano bar upstairs, as well as toilets that are historic monuments of Art Nouveau, with sculpted oak woodwork and porcelain wash basins.

Fitzgerald and Hemingway shared a long lunch here before meeting Morley Callaghan, a Canadian writer and amateur boxer, for a work-out. Fitzgerald served as timekeeper as Hemingway and Callaghan boxed. After one very long round, Callaghan knocked Hemingway to his knees, and a startled Fitzgerald blurted out his mistake in letting the round go past two minutes. Hemingway was unforgiving, even after the three men adjourned to the Falstaff for drinks.

Right Bank Literary Bars

PRESUMABLY F. Scott Fitzgerald once said to Robert Benchley, "Bob, don't you know that drinking is slow death?" Benchley, so the story goes, responded, "So who's in a hurry?" Both men enjoyed drinking in the bars of hotels: Benchley at the Algonquin in New York, Fitzgerald at the Ritz in Paris. Both, I am sorry to relate, were indeed hurried to their deaths by this habit.

In a city of cafés, a few Parisian bars have nevertheless been important to literature and writers. Jake Barnes in Hemingway's *The Sun Also Rises* often stopped by the bar at the Hôtel Crillon in the Place de la Concorde, thought to be the longest bar in Europe until it was dismantled in 1984 to make room for a restaurant. The Hole in the Wall Bar (23 Boulevard des Capucines) closed in 1988, but it was once the hangout of young writers working in the newspaper offices around the Opéra during the first decades of this century. Hemingway called it "a hangout for deserters and for dope peddlers during and after the first war," presumably because a rear exit opened into the infamous sewers of Paris.

But other bars with literary associations continue to pour drinks. The bar in the exclusive, arty little L'Hôtel, 13 Rue des Beaux-Arts, where Oscar Wilde died in November, 1900, serves visiting writers as well as artists such as Mick Jagger. Two other hotel bars, at the Ritz and the Pont-Royal (see the St-Germain-des-Prés section), deserve special attention.

A watering place made famous by Fitzgerald and wealthy Americans of the 1920s—and later by Ernest Hemingway—is the Hôtel Ritz bar, scene of lavish parties before the Depression.

Hemingway claimed to have "liberated" the Ritz when he arrived in 1944 at the end of the war with a band of dusty soldiers and ordered 93 dry martinis. He held court then and later, entertaining Marlene Dietrich, Jean-Paul Sartre and dozens of other celebrities. In tribute to the fame that he brought the hotel and his friendship with Charles Ritz, the latter renamed the smaller of the hotel bars (formerly the ladies' bar) the Hemingway Bar. It is just inside the Rue Cambon door to the right.

The best literary use of the Ritz bar is in the works of Fitzgerald: it is Abe North's favorite drinking spot in *Tender Is the Night* and the setting for "The Bridal Party" and "News of Paris—Fifteen Years Ago." In "Babylon Revisited," Charlie Wales returns to Paris in the 1930s to find the "stillness in the Ritz bar . . . strange and portentous." It is no longer an American bar, he laments, it has "gone back into France."

Harry's New York Bar is like an ivy-league English pub. Through the swinging doors is a long bar to the left and college banners along the dark wood walls in the back. Hemingway dropped in here off and on for forty years; owner Harry MacElhone served as his second when he boxed in the 1920s. Fitzgerald drank to excess many nights here, and one legend has him taken home dead drunk in a commandeered hearse. George Gershwin used to bang away at *An American In Paris* downstairs, and the customers complained about the "piano-tuning session."

It was called New York Bar when it was founded in 1911, making it "the oldest cocktail bar in Europe." The name Harry's was added in 1923 when MacElhone took over (one source says he bought it in 1927). His son, Andy, who played with Jack Hemingway when their fathers were absorbed in boxing, took over from his father. Harry's grandson, Duncan, now runs the bar where the Bloody Mary, the Side Car and a half dozen other drinks were invented. American and English sportsmen and businessmen are at home here with the ivy-league banners and the fishing and hunting photographs of Hemingway on the wall. "Sank Roo Doe Noo" on the front door unashamedly tells monolingual English-speaking customers what to instruct their taxi drivers when they want to come back. Among the dozens of writers who have dropped into this bar during its 80-year history are Thornton Wilder, James Jones, Brendan Behan, and Liam O'Flaherty. The bar appears in numerous fictional accounts of its customers, including the James Bond novels of Ian Fleming and *Dodsworth* by Sinclair Lewis.

HEMINGWAY BAR AT THE HÔTEL RITZ
38 Rue Cambon, one block west of Place Vendome (1e)
Tel: 42.60.38.30
Open: 11 a.m. to 1 a.m.
Métro: Madeleine

HARRY'S NEW YORK BAR
5 Rue Daunou, between Rue de la Paix and Avenue de l'Opéra (2e)
Tel: 42.61.71.14
Open: every day from 10 a.m. to 4 a.m.
Métro: Opéra

Cabarets

THOUGH THE ORIGIN of the word *cabaret* is not known, it has been around since the 14th century when ground-level stores sold wine and spirits. Cabarets and taverns were thought of as sinful places of gambling, brawling and prostitution. Though cafés have surpassed them in popularity, with their windows and mirrors, marble tables and coffee, cabarets still exist in Paris. Today's cabarets feature entertainment, folk or political music, and satire.

The first famous cabarets were in Montmartre. Café de la Nouvelle Athènes is where Degas, Renoir and Pissaro discussed art in the 1870s and 1880s, and where later Satie played the piano. The most famous cabaret was the Chat Noir, which Roger Shattuck says was "a *salon* stood on its head," with the waiters in the dress of the Académie Française; where the Hydropathes, Latin Quarter poets, painters and *chansonniers,* recited, sang and issued a newspaper; and where crazy demonstrators mocked their own era. Though the Chat Noir closed in 1897, Le Lapin Agile, the birthplace of Cubism, remains. Lapin Agile, founded in 1860, is housed in a small cottage behind a twisted-tree fence. Utrillo painted it many times, and Picasso, Modigliani, Apollinaire and Max Jacob hung out here. If you come very late, early morning that is, you may be able to catch the spirit of the old cabaret.

LE LAPIN AGILE
22 Rue des Saules (18e) Tel: 46.06.85.87
Open: 9 p.m. to 2 a.m., entry 90 francs
(closed Monday)
Métro: Lamarck Caulaincourt

Basic Café Vocabulary

Establishments

American bar: a bar that has an area for sitting at tables.

Bistro(t): originally a wine-tasting bar, now it usually means an informal, family run eating place with a bar toward the front.

Bistro à vin: a wine bar that offers carefully chosen wines by the glass or bottle and platters of cheese, charcuterie (cold cuts), pâté and sandwiches in a casual setting.

Brasserie: all-day eating, beer on tap, usually large and well-lighted, featuring inexpensive Alsatian or country food such as choucroute (sauerkraut), cassoulet (white bean stew), sausage and potatoes.

Cabaret: a drinking place that features music, dancing, group singing, with an emphasis on pleasure and relaxation in the evening.

Café: a meeting place for exchange of social and intellectual information, serving snacks, coffee and alcohol, often with a terrace that opens out onto the sidewalk. Usually opens at 8 a.m.

Café-tabac: a café that sells tobacco and stamps at the bar.

Crémerie: a cheap eating establishment that sells milk, eggs, cheese and dishes made from them. Most crémeries have become restaurants with larger menus.

Restaurant: serves lunch and dinner, usually opened by 1 p.m. for lunch and 8 p.m. for dinner.

Salon de thé: a tearoom that also offers tarts, chocolates, pastries and sandwiches in a calm and cozy atmosphere.

Popular Drinks

Anis: a strongly flavored herb drink.

Café: coffee.
    Café noir or café express: plain strong black coffee.
    Café serré: extra strong (half the water).

Café: coffee (continued)

    Café allongé: weak, often served with a small pitcher of hot water.

    Café crème: expresso with steamed milk, occasionally with whipped cream.

    Café au lait: expresso with hot milk, the preferred French breakfast drink.

    Café glacé: iced coffee.

    Double express: double expresso.

    Déca or décaféiné: decaffeinated coffee.

Chocolat chaud: hot chocolate.

Eau: water.

    Une carafe d'eau: tap water.

    Perrier: the most popular mineral water, with bubbles (*gazeuse*).

Orangina: carbonated orange soda, the most popular non-alcoholic café drink.

Schweppes: tonic water, carbonated.

Thé: tea.

    Thé nature: plain.

    Thé au lait: with milk.

    Thé citron: with lemon.

    Infusion: herbal tea.

Vin: wine.

    Vin blanc: white wine.

    Vin rouge: red wine.

    Kir: white wine with crème de cassis, a liqueur made of black currant berries.

    Kir royal: champagne with crème de cassis or crème de framboise.

Snacks

Baguette: a long, narrow loaf of bread.

Charcuterie: sausage, pâté, prepared meats.

Croissant: flaky crescent-shaped roll.

Croque-monsieur: grilled ham and cheese sandwich.

Croque-madame: open-faced grilled ham and cheese sandwich with fried egg "sunny side up."

Crudités: variety of raw vegetables, usually grated carrots, beets, sliced tomatoes.

Jambon: cooked ham.

Oeuf dur: hard-boiled egg.

Pain Poilâne: brown bread with a thick crust, considered the best bread in Paris.

Pâté: a sliced loaf of ground, pressed meat, usually including liver.

Sandwich mixte: buttered baguette filled with Gruyère cheese and thin slices of ham.

Tips

If you are only having a drink, sit at a bare table. A cloth or paper placemat means the table is reserved for dining.

The tip (*service,* from 12 to 15 percent) is always included in the price. You do not have to pay more.

Opening and closing hours will vary with the season. Most French businesses close during July or August.

Further Reading

Boettcher, Jurgen, ed. *Coffee Houses of Europe.* London: Thames and Hudson, 1980.

Cafés, Bistros et Compagnie. Expositions itinérantes CCI, No. 4 Centre Georges-Pompidou, Paris, 1977.

Diwo, Jean. *Chez Lipp.* Paris: Denoël, 1981.

Ellis, Aytoun. *The Penny Universities: A History of the Coffee Houses.* London: Secker & Warburg, 1956.

Fargue, Léon-Paul. *Le Piéton de Paris.* Paris: Gallimard, 1932.

Fitch, Noël Riley. *Hemingway in Paris: Walks for the Literary Traveller.* London: Thorsons, 1989.

——————. *Sylvia Beach & the Lost Generation: A History of Literary Paris in the Twenties and Thirties.* New York: W. W. Norton, 1983.

Hemingway, Ernest. *A Moveable Feast.* New York: Scribners, 1964.

Huddleston, Sisley. *Paris Salons, Cafés, Studios: Being Social, Artistic and Literary Memories.* Philadelphia: J. B. Lippincott, 1928.

Lemaire, Gérard-George. *Les cafés littéraires.* Paris: Editions Henry Veyrier, 1987.

Littlewood, Ian. *Paris: A Literary Companion.* London: John Murray, 1987.

Lottman, Herbert R. "Splendors and Miseries of the Literary Cafés." *Saturday Review,* 48 (13 March 1965), 34–35, 119–21.

Malki-Thouvenel, Beatrice. *Cabarets, Cafés et Bistrots de Paris.* Paris: Editions Horwath, 1987.

Planiol, Française. *La Coupole: 60 ans de Montparnasse.* Paris: Denoël, 1986.

Root, Waverley. "Brasserie Lipp—Rendezvous for le tout Paris." *Holiday,* 46 (October 1969), 66–67, 94.

Seigel, Jerrold. *Bohemian Paris: Culture, Politics, and the Boundaries of Bourgeois Life, 1830–1930.* New York: Viking, 1986.

Shattuck, Roger. *The Banquet Years: The Origins of the Avant Garde in France, 1885 to World War I.* New York: Random House, 1968.

Trabant, Warren & Jean. *Paris Confidential.* Baltimore: Agora, 1987.

Villefosse, René Héron de. *Histoire et Géographie Gourmandes de Paris.* Les Editions of Paris, 1956.

Wells, Patricia. *Food Lover's Guide to Paris.* New York: Workman, 1990.

Index